CHILDREN OF PROMISE

The Case for Baptizing Infants

by

Geoffrey W. Bromiley

WILLIAM B. EERDMANS PUBLISHING COMPANY
GRAND RAPIDS, MICHIGAN

Library of Congress Cataloging in Publication Data

Bromiley, Geoffrey William.
   Children of promise.

   Includes index.
   1.   Infant baptism.   I.   Title.
BV813.2.B76   265'.12   79-10346
ISBN 0-8028-1797-1

For James and Stephen

Contents

Preface

IN ITS FIRST EDITION this little book was hastily written and published to meet a particular situation. Across the years, however, it served a more general, if modest, purpose. When it finally dropped out of circulation, many requests came for its reissue in a better format, the more so as the occasion of its composition perpetuates itself with only trifling changes. This is why a new edition has been prepared.

With a new edition the question of revision and expansion inevitably arose. The decision has been taken, however, to make only some minor emendations and add a little to the biblical material. To do more, especially in the way of detailed exegetical or historical discussion, would be to change the character and intention of the work. Those who want access to the historical debate might consult the chapter on "Baptism and Anabaptism" in my *Historical Theology: An Introduction*. The present book is a simple attempt, in generally intelligible terms, to get at the biblical understanding which underlies the continuation of infant baptism in many of the evangelical churches.

Thanks are due to those who have commented favorably or more critically on the first edition, to those who have urged its republication, and to the publishers who have made the present edition possible. It is sent out, not in the hope of winning a debate, but with the prayer that God may be glorified both in continued reflection on baptism and also in its administration, whether to young or old.

G. W. BROMILEY

Pasadena, Epiphany 1979

Introduction

INFANT BAPTISM constitutes a problem for many members of the Reformation churches, especially for those in the early days of Christian experience who come to a personal commitment during schooldays or at college. The new convert does not always see easily the relevance and meaning of earlier baptism or indeed of whatever instruction follows it. He or she may feel a need to make some dramatic confession of the new faith in an act of rebaptism as the first real baptism. The challenge of Baptist teaching, with its apparently solid backing in the New Testament, will inevitably be encountered and may have an unsettling influence. Not having the time or training to weigh the matter thoroughly, the new convert may be swept away by the supposedly convincing arguments of critical friends, or may reject rebaptism only with a bad conscience and a hampering sense of perplexity, or may indeed take refuge in the idea that here is only a matter of divergent practice with no theological significance. In these circumstances the need arises for a short but comprehensive statement of the biblical reasons for infant baptism. The present booklet tries to meet that need.

The purpose of this work will indicate clearly that it is neither polemical in character nor deliberately proselytizing in intention. No great energy will be expended on the negative process of analyzing, comparing, and triumphantly demolishing the teachings of those who differ. Naturally some Baptist counterarguments will have to be considered and the reasons for their rejection stated. Naturally, too, it is hoped that those who do not accept infant baptism will read the statement and consider it calmly and carefully in the light of Holy Scripture and the context of scriptural doctrine. Much of the acrimony which has regrettably entered into the discussion of this issue undoubtedly derives from an unwillingness to subject presuppositions to such solid biblical investigation, resulting in intolerance on the one hand and exclusivism on the other. Obviously this is wrong. What is needed is that both those who baptize infants and those who do not be prepared for mutual toleration and respect, and, if necessary, for agreement to disagree.

The statement which follows is, of course, a brief and summarized account of the matter as the main evangelical churches of the Reformation see it. Clearly, the various theologians of the Reformation confessions will develop their basic considerations differently. The individual differences will not be considered here, however, for fundamentally they are of no more significance than the variations in Protestantism with which some older Roman Catholic theologians have foolishly tried to discredit essential Protestant teaching. Nor has it been thought necessary to fill out the picture with exegetical, historical, or dogmatic details. The important thing is that members of the Reformation churches, no matter when their individual commitment to Christ is made, should not abandon their baptism without considering the points made here, even though it is all to the good that they look at the Baptist alternative to learn what is to be learned there. It is also important that Baptists realize that the historic practice rests, not on convention or convenience alone, nor merely on church legislation, but on a very definite biblical and evangelical understanding which they should respect even if they do accept.

In consonance with the purpose and spirit of the work, critical comments will be welcomed. They ought not to be advanced, however, merely to score debating points. They should aim at a better discernment of God's will in the understanding and administration of the sacrament or ordinance which he himself has appointed.

I
The Practice of the New Testament

THE CHIEF DIFFICULTY in relation to the New Testament is that it does not give us the plain and direct evidence for or against infant baptism which most people desire and which many think they find in it. In the baptismal command incorporated in the Great Commission, Jesus neither told his apostles specifically to baptize infants nor specifically forbad them to do so. Similarly the few accounts we have of apostolic baptisms do not actually say that infants were baptized nor do they tell us that infants were excluded. If direct evidence were available, whether of precept or precedent, the debate could hardly continue, and indeed would never have arisen in the first place.

The silence of the New Testament can be taken in two ways. On the one hand the inference is drawn that since we do have accounts of adult converts this must be the exclusive rule. The problem here, of course, is not with the fact but with the conclusion. Never in the long and varied course of its history has the church denied that adult converts should be baptized as in the New Testament. In the missionary situation of the early church, when so many were being won to Christ out of paganism, adults were constantly baptized and the catechetical courses culminated in the great baptismal administrations at Easter and Pentecost. Similarly, whenever the church has seriously discharged its ministry of evangelism, it has baptized the adults who constitute the first generation of Christian converts. The fact is incontestable, but can one derive from the fact an exclusive rule?

Against this inference it is argued that the inclusion of the children of adult converts is so much in line with the thought and practice of the Old Testament that it is taken for granted in the New, as the household baptisms of Acts suggest even if they do not prove. In this regard the unity of the Old and New Testaments has an importance which should not be overlooked, though in the first instance it may mean simply that the apostles who first administered Christian baptism were steeped in the theological teaching of the first revelation of God to Israel.

Now in favor of the first conclusion and against the second it is a sound principle that what is not explicitly stated should not be too easily assumed. Many medieval innovations both in doctrine and practice depended upon New Testament silences which were filled in with the help of arbitrary human imagination and supposed apostolic tradition. It must be conceded that even the accounts of household baptisms do not expressly state that small children were included in any given instance. In these circumstances, is it not wiser and safer to keep to what we are explicitly told in the New Testament? Do we not do better to see every situation as basically a missionary situation and to make every baptism an adult baptism on suitable profession of personal faith? That is the Baptist contention reduced to its barest essentials.

The conclusion is not unreasonable. Before we rush into it, however, there are three things that we do well to remember. 1. The first is that there are incontestable cases where the silences of the New Testament may be filled in by way of legitimate inference. The classic example is still the best. From the church's very beginning women have been admitted to the Lord's table on equal terms with men. But no explicit text for this can be found. When Christ instituted the Lord's Supper he did not command any women to "do this." In the few records we have of New Testament communions there is no express reference to women having been present and participating. If no responsible body of Christian opinion has ever held that women ought to be excluded from the Lord's table, it is not on the ground of any specific support in precept or practice but on the ground of legitimate inference. This being so, the similar lack of an express commandment or example does not in itself constitute a decisive reason against admitting infants to baptism.

2. The second point is that some external evidence exists that the disciples would and did take baptism to apply to the children of converted and confessing adults. This need not be presented in detail, for it is much debated and is in any case only incidental to the main discussion. Its value, if any, is corroborative. This does not mean, however, that it should be dismissed altogether. It takes two main forms.

The first is that from the first century of the Christian era the Jews themselves practiced baptism as a rite for the initiation of proselytes which definitely included children along with their parents. Whether Christian or Jewish baptism came first need not concern us. Nor does it matter that Jewish proselyte baptism was a once-for-all act not applying to future generations. What we learn from the rite is simply the way in which the covenant people of the Old Testament viewed the relation of parent and child in covenant initiation.

The second form of external evidence is the testimony to infant baptism and its apostolic origin which comes from the second half of the second century through the beginning of the third century in the early Christian writers Irenaeus and Origen. This, of course, leaves a century or more of silence which can again be assessed in different ways. But even in the comparatively scanty literature of the intervening period there are possible references, as in Justin Martyr. Furthermore, in the case of Irenaeus we are probably only in the third generation after the apostles, for Irenaeus claimed to be a hearer of Polycarp and Polycarp of the apostle John. A collection of patristic references or possible allusions may be found in the two volumes of the older but still useful work of W. Wall, *The History of Infant Baptism*.

3. The third thing to be remembered is the one that really counts. Upon this, therefore, the main stress must be placed. It is that, quite apart from the external evidence, the New Testament itself offers plain indications that the children of Christians are regarded as members of the divine community just as the children of Old Testament Israel were. In these circumstances the inference of an accepted practice of infant baptism is undoubtedly legitimate if not absolutely or bindingly so. Indeed, we may put it more strongly than that. The indications are so clear and widespread that, as in the case of women communicants,

4

the onus of proof really falls on those who wish to deny the practice because of the lack of an express command, statement, or precedent in the New Testament. We must now look at these indications in more detail.

The first is the attitude and statements of Jesus to and about children in the course of his earthly ministry. It must be recalled that we are not seeking a direct reference to baptism. Nor is it to be forgotten that in a verse like Matthew 18:3 our Lord draws from childhood the lesson of the new birth of adults as the children of God. The most interesting and significant thing, however, is that the Lord Jesus Christ has a concern for children, not merely as living parables, but as they are in themselves. Thus he receives children into his arms and blesses them.[1] He is angry with his disciples, and rebukes them when they try to keep the children from him.[2] He tells us—a hard truth for proud adults—that the things of God are hidden from the wise and prudent and revealed to babes.[3] He takes up the statement of the psalmist[4] that out of the mouths of babes and sucklings God has perfected praise.[5] He does not seem to share the rationalistic view that the Holy Spirit cannot do his work of illumination and regeneration except in those who have at least the beginnings of an adult understanding. He does not endorse the idea that small children are not proper subjects of his kingdom and therefore of the sacraments or signs of the kingdom. Indeed he speaks very solemnly and forthrightly about "lit-

[1]Matthew 19:13–15; Mark 10:13–16; Luke 18:15–17
[2]Mark 10:14
[3]Luke 10:21
[4]Psalm 8:2
[5]Matthew 21:16

tle ones which believe in me" against whom we offend at our peril.[6] A saying repeated in the first three Gospels is equally firm and definite: "Of such is the kingdom of heaven."[7]

When we turn from our Lord's own ministry to that of the apostles in Acts, no express reference is made to infants or small children as such. As noted, however, it very quickly appears that in many cases not just isolated individuals but also whole households received the first baptisms.[8] The number of reported instances is not large but there is no reason to suppose that they were exceptional. In the example of the Philippian jailor it is possible that all the members of the household came to personal faith, although the text does not specifically state that each individually believed and made a personal confession.[9] In the instance of Cornelius, one might infer from the account that all who were baptized were of an age to hear the gospel.[10] Yet oddly enough we are not told anything about faith or the confession of faith. What calls for notice is endowment with the Holy Spirit. This, of course, would bring faith with it but plainly did not lie within the range of human possibilities, whether infant or adult. It was miraculous in character—a mighty act of God.

In at least two other cases, that of Lydia[11] and that of Stephanas,[12] no mention at all is made of individual faith on the part of all the members of the baptized households.

[6] Matthew 18:6
[7] Matthew 19:14; cf. Mark 10:14; Luke 18:16
[8] From Acts 10:34–48
[9] Acts 16:34
[10] Acts 10:34–48
[11] Acts 16:14–15
[12] 1 Corinthians 1:16

Whether or not these households included children we have, of course, no means of determining. Lydia seems to have been the head of the household as well as the business yet we cannot say she never married. She could very well have been a widow and a mother or even a grandmother. The record shows no interest in such matters, since it is not given us to solve our problems about infant baptism. The detailed domestic circumstances of Stephanas are no less obscure. What matters for our purpose is that in these accounts we have distinct examples of an apostolic practice of household baptism. In view of contemporary Jewish thinking, and even more so of the teaching and actions of Christ himself, it becomes difficult to imagine that when these households did contain infants or small children the apostles would deliberately exclude them from baptism. In this connection it is not irrelevant that in the first gospel appeal in Acts 2 the apostle Peter makes it plain that the word and work of God are still covenantal in scope: "The promise is to you, and to your children, and to all that are afar off, as many as the Lord our God shall call."[13] We shall see the full force of this only when we listen to the voice of the Old Testament which it so clearly echoes.

The Epistles carry us a stage further along this line of thinking. In 1 Corinthians 7 Paul comes up against the difficult question of marriages which have become "mixed" with the conversion of one of the partners from paganism (or possibly Judaism). If the unbelieving spouse will not continue the marriage, then nothing can be done and the general prohibition of divorce no longer applies. On the other hand, the believing partner must not take an

[13]Acts 2:39

initiative in separation. Why not? According to Paul a principle of great importance covers these cases, although we must be careful not to extend it to mixed marriages which are contracted deliberately and unnecessarily. This principle is that the unbelieving partner is "sanctified" by the believing husband or wife, and therefore the children of such a marriage are not unclean but "holy."[14] In relation to the unbelieving spouse the apostle's meaning seems to be that in virtue of the other's faith he or she is separated to God, enjoys a status within the covenant, and comes into the sphere of evangelical action and promise with a hope of future conversion. But the same is true of the children. (How much more so, one might suppose, when both the parents are confessing Christians.)

To avoid this conclusion is very difficult, for what else can Paul mean? It is obviously fanciful to think that he has personal holiness of character or conduct in view. At the opposite extreme he can hardly be referring to civil legitimacy, for in the eyes of the law the children of a properly contracted marriage are legitimate irrespective of the Christian belief or unbelief of the parents. On the other hand, if Paul has a kind of ecclesiastical legitimacy in mind, or legitimacy in the eyes of God, this implies legitimacy within the covenant people, which brings us back to the original conclusion. In other words, the children are recognized as having a status within the covenant, to be holy in this sense, so long as either parent is a professing member of the covenant people.

To anticipate a little, one may already wonder, if covenant membership is thus acknowledged, why the sign of the covenant should be denied unless the older children

[14] I Corinthians 7:14

themselves, or the younger children's parents, are unwilling that it should be given. If, of course, the unbelieving parent is unwilling, then baptism might very well not be administered. This happened not infrequently in the earlier days of the Christian mission. If both parents are believers, however, the question of unwillingness need hardly arise and there is thus no obstacle to the receiving of the covenant sign by children who already have covenant holiness. It need occasion little surprise that many parents who will not permit infant baptism try to give expression to the truth in all this by substituting a service of infant dedication. But in the New Testament there is no precept or precedent for a service of this kind. Nor indeed is dedication the same thing as covenant separation. The Old Testament offers no help in this regard. One might indeed dedicate a child to God as Samuel was dedicated for special service, possibly as a Nazarite.[15] But in the Old Testament a child dedicated in this way had already received infant circumcision, which God himself had appointed to be the sign of covenant separation and status.

In addition to the important verse in 1 Corinthians 7 we should also notice that the Epistles apparently presuppose that children are members of the church. For example, both Ephesians[16] and Colossians[17] contain short admonitions to children. Similarly 1 John[18] has a threefold exhortation to older people, younger people, and children. Sometimes in this Epistle all members of the community seem to be referred to as little children.[19] When

[15] 1 Samuel 1:21–28
[16] Ephesians 6:1
[17] Colossians 3:20
[18] 1 John 2:13
[19] 1 John 2:18; 5:21

this occurs, the reference could be to their spiritual immaturity, or to the fact that the author is their father in Christ. In the threefold exhortation, too, it is not impossible that the reference might be to stages in spiritual growth. It seems more natural, however, to take it that the apostle is thinking in terms of physical age groups, so that the church includes children in years as well as in faith. In the case of the Pauline Epistles, the writer is obviously stating a general duty to parents which applies to adult children as well, that is, to all those who have parents still alive. It could also be suggested that the exhortation has value only for those children who are old enough to have made, or to make, a responsible decision of faith. The text itself, however, includes no specific qualifications of this sort. The obvious interpretation of the passage is that the apostle is admonishing all children within the covenant and congregation to fulfill the specific duty of obedience to parents. This includes adult children and all children who have come to faith, whether with their parents or without them. Yet one cannot stop there. It is addressed as well to the children of Christian parentage growing up within the covenant who are numbered among the "saints" because from the very first they are separated to God and holy. If this is so, then clearly all the children of Christians, belonging to the holy community, and marked with the distinctive sign of the covenant, are to be taught from their infancy the covenant responsibility and privilege of obedience to parents in the Lord.

Whether taken individually or together, these considerations do not amount to an absolute and compelling reason for baptizing infants. As we have seen at the outset, the whole difficulty in this matter lies in the lack of explicit and exclusive direction pointing either way.

There is no specific command either to baptize or not to baptize infants. There is no specific mention of an infant being baptized in the household of Acts, yet there is no specific statement that these households contained no infants, or if they did that the infants were excluded from baptism. Indeed, we have no explicit instance of the child of a believer coming to faith and then being baptized, as in a good deal of Baptist practice. The three points advanced cannot take the place of the direct evidence which we lack. On the other hand, they are not on that account to be rejected as worthless. What we learn from them is that within the context of the thinking and utterance of the New Testament it is possible and even natural to view children as being from infancy members of Christ's kingdom, and consequently to accord them a definite covenant standing. This being so, it is difficult to see how the disciples could have thought that prior to individual conversion infants should be grouped as outsiders, and thus denied the ordinance or sacrament of baptism.

2
The Witness of the Old Testament

IN OUR DISCUSSION of New Testament practice we have already been led to think and speak in substantially Old Testament terms. The ideas of the holy community, the covenant people, and the covenant sign all go back deep into the Old Testament. It is not surprising, of course, that there should be this recurrence in the New Testament. Christ did not come, nor did Christian faith arise, in a vacuum. A particular background and context had been prepared. Our Lord and the disciples already had the word of God. They were steeped in it, and they appealed to it. They were not setting it aside but consciously fulfilling it. The word of God was for them the Old Testament. It is therefore necessary and right that we set against the background of the Old Testament, not only the message and mission of Christ himself, but also that of the apostles whom he chose and commissioned to preach the gospel and administer the sacraments.

We must not be misled at this point by any form of either rationalistic or evangelical dissection of the Bible.

Taught by our Lord and the New Testament authors, the church has maintained across the centuries a testimony to the unity of scripture. Nevertheless, pressure has always been brought to bear on this position from the days of Marcion and the Gnostics. The witness of the Old Testament can be played down in more ways than one. A certain type of biblical criticism dismisses or relativizes the teaching and practice of the Old Testament as a lower and outmoded form of religious development. In this case, of course, the New Testament might suffer the same fate when arrogantly—and ironically—measured against the achievements of modern thought and conduct. Those who resist these critical extremes, however, may easily fall victim to the dispensationalists, or to certain advocates of progressive revelation who see in the Old Testament, and often enough in parts of the New Testament, words of God which have no direct relevance to the church age, or to the final period of revelation, and consequently to believers today. In this connection it is not without interest that the Anabaptists, the sixteenth-century precursors of the Baptists, had a marked tendency to disparage the Old Testament and to destroy the proper unity of scripture except along the lines of a wholesale spiritualizing. Even some who have no desire to go the ways of rationalism, dispensationalism, or progressive revelation, may sometimes lay such emphasis on the difference between law and gospel that they lose sight of the higher unity of the divine word and purpose. This does not matter so much, however, for, as we shall see, the Old Testament covenant and its sign predate the law. Paul points out in Romans[1] that the promise and the sign of the promise were in fact

---

[1]Romans 4:13–14; cf. also Galatians 3:17–18 and Luke 1:55, 72–73

given to Abraham four hundred years before the promul-
gation of the law at Sinai. Yet any weakening of the close
relatedness of the Old and New Testaments can have
dangerous consequences. This is distinctly brought to
light in the present-day tendency to strip off huge chunks
of scripture on the ground that they are timebound in
expression or in mode of thinking.

It is not to be disputed, of course, that differences do
exist between the old covenant, or the old form of the
covenant, and the new. Christians have always understood
that a good deal of the Old Testament, and especially of
the Old Testament legislation, no longer applies directly
to the Christian community or the individual Christian.
All the same, the greatest care is needed in stating the
difference, for Jesus himself told us that the law was not to
be destroyed but fulfilled, and that not one jot or tittle
would be removed from it prior to the fulfillment.[2] The
basic distinction must not be regarded as that of two oppo-
sites, nor as that of a lower and a higher dispensation that
replaces it. It is to be viewed instead as the distinction
between a promise and the redemption which supersedes
it, or a type and the reality into which it is taken up. The
old covenant is the covenant of promise and the new covenant is the covenant of fulfilled promise. Fundamentally, however, this covenant is one, just as the purpose,
word, and work of God are one. The Old Testament is
superseded by the New only in the sense that it is fulfilled
in the New. The external details differ but not at the
expense of the underlying consistency or continuity of the
divine action, message, and command. Hence the Old
Testament cannot properly be understood apart from the

[2]Matthew 5:17–18; cf. Romans 3:31, etc.

New, but equally the New Testament cannot be understood apart from the Old. In this regard Calvin's discussion of the similarity and difference of the Testaments in *Institutes* II, x–xi might still be consulted with profit.

In connection with baptism an illustration of the interrelationship is found at once, for the New Testament itself points us to two "types" of Christian baptism in Old Testament incidents. It is tempting to look for other types as well, as, for instance, the crossing of the Jordan or the cleansing of Naaman the leper. These events undoubtedly have great edificatory value, and so long as due caution is exercised may be given a valid homiletical application. Nevertheless, no dogmatic significance can be attached to them in baptismal theology. The situation differs, however, when we come to the two pictures that are singled out by the two leading apostles, the ark by Peter[3] and the cloud and the Red Sea by Paul.[4] Both these types bring out the very intimate relation between the Old Testament and the New. Both of them, as types of baptism, have a very significant bearing on the topic under discussion.

It is hardly necessary to do more than indicate the main and obvious parallels. The theme is everywhere the great biblical theme of salvation in the midst of, and almost, as it were, in spite of and by way of divine judgment. What is pictured is the deliverance of an elect family or people. The motif of the covenant is prominent in both incidents. In the first we have the covenant of God with Noah. His family is included, enabling him to become the progenitor of a new race. In the second the

[3] I Peter 3:20–21
[4] I Corinthians 10:1–2

15

deliverance leads to a new covenant relation between God and Israel, but it is premised on the prior covenant with Abraham. This comes to fulfillment in the redemption and calling of Abraham's physical progeny by Isaac and Jacob and aims at the promised seed in whom all the nations will be blessed. In both instances, too, we find that the saving work of God is accompanied by the offering of sacrifice, the burnt offering of Noah when he came out of the ark, and the sacrifice of the Passover prior to the Exodus and the Red Sea deliverance.[5] But this is a subject in itself.

What concerns us at the moment is the subsidiary but substantial fact that in both these typical incidents the covenant is made not with the individual alone, with Noah or Moses, but with the family or people. Not Noah alone but his wife, his sons, and his sons' wives are brought into the ark and preserved there.[6] Not Moses alone, nor just the male Israelites, but all the children of Israel, the men, their wives, and their little ones, go out from Egypt and walk on dry land across the sea.[7] The point is not merely that in these actions, which are types of baptism, the children share the experience with their parents. It is rather that the covenantal action of God is not with individuals in isolation, but with families, or with individuals in families, so that those belonging to the individuals are also separated as the people of God and in a very special sense come within the sphere of the divine covenant. If, of course, these pictures had merely been chosen at random, it would probably be fanciful to emphasize or even

[5]Genesis 8:20; Exodus 12
[6]Genesis 7:7
[7]Exodus 14:13

to mention points of this kind. But this is not so either materially or formally. Materially the incidents which are chosen as types form an important part of the work of God in the Old Testament and display the essential characteristics of this work. Formally the doctrine of scripture means that the incidents are not, as it were, picked out of a hat by Peter and Paul but selected by the Holy Spirit through these apostolic witnesses. Hence we do well not to overlook these significant aspects of the matter. Indeed, very strong reasons are needed if we are going to believe that the family relationship of this type has been completely set aside and even reversed in the New Testament fulfillment.

But there is much more to it than that. For when we probe more deeply into the New Testament we find that baptism as the sign of the new covenant takes the place of circumcision as the sign of the old covenant. Even a cursory reading of the entire Bible shows clearly enough that the so-called sacraments instituted by Christ, baptism and the Lord's Supper, correspond in a very striking way to the two covenantal signs of the Old Testament, the Lord's Supper to the Passover and baptism to circumcision.

The main difference between the old signs and the new is evident at once and explains the replacement. For the earlier signs both involve the shedding of blood and point forward prophetically and typologically to the shedding of the blood of Christ in his vicarious work of reconciliation. In contrast the new signs are without blood, for they now look backward apostolically to the one sacrifice for sins which has rendered all further shedding of blood unnecessary.[8]

[8]Hebrews 10:12

Notwithstanding the difference, the correlation of the signs plainly belongs to the very substance of the biblical teaching and indeed of the divine work which is its theme and center. It is also brought out very specifically in the text of the New Testament itself.

In the case of the Passover and the Lord's Supper the correlation may be found in the institution. The Lord gave the sign of the new covenant at the very time when he was observing for the last time the sign of the old. He did so in words which left no room for reasonable doubt as to his meaning. The Passover ceased to be obligatory for Christians because, as Paul put it so well, Christ our Passover is sacrificed for us.[9] The prophetic sign has come to fulfillment and the apostolic sign, the remembrance of Christ's death and passion in the bread and the cup, has become a perpetual celebration in the church.

In the case of circumcision and baptism the connection is made by the apostolic writer in Colossians 2:11–12. This passage has been variously expounded in detail but the central truth which it proclaims is surely perspicuous enough. Both circumcision and baptism have the same inner significance. They both refer to the circumcision without hands which we now have in Jesus Christ. The basic continuity of significance establishes the close relationship between the old sign and the new even though, like the Passover and the Lord's Supper, they differ so much externally.

The continuity or equation which may be seen here is important for two reasons. 1. In the first place we recall, according to the institution of circumcision in Genesis 17, that when the household of Abraham was circumcised

[9] 1 Corinthians 5:7

18

along with Abraham, circumcision was henceforward to be administered on the eighth day to all male children within the covenant family. Now perhaps it is rather over-fanciful to discern in the eighth day a forward look to the day of the new creation which will later be the Lord's day. It is no fancy, however, to find the witness of circumcision to be wholly of a piece with that of the two New Testament types of baptism, the ark and the Red Sea passage. For again children are included with their parents in the separation as a covenant people and therefore in the covenant sign. God does not deal with the individual in isolation, but with the individual in a family or people.

It will be objected, of course, that circumcision, in contrast to the ark and the Exodus, applies only to the male children of the covenant people, whereas Christian baptism is intended in its range and compass to include both males and females, who are all one in Christ Jesus.[10] Here, of course, is one of the points of discontinuity within the continuity, just as the extension of both baptism and the Lord's Supper to all nations is another point of discontinuity. But why does this discontinuity exist if an equation may be made? This poses a good question, for here we also have a discontinuity within the Old Testament itself. Girls were undoubtedly redeemed out of Egypt as well as boys, and women no less than men belonged to the covenant people of Israel. Why, then, should this covenant sign have from the very first a male restriction?

In reply two things should be noted. First, this question exists whether or not baptism is seen as a replacement for and fulfillment of circumcision. Second, scripture does

[10]Galatians 3:28

19

not specifically raise or answer the question but simply records the facts. Hence one might state with some justice that the continuity of circumcision and baptism does not depend on an explanation being given. Nevertheless, it might be profitable to take the matter a little further.

On a more slipshod view of scripture one might simply appeal to the timebound nature of biblical signs and practices. God in instituting circumcision and baptism simply used whatever materials were at hand. Thus no great importance is to be attached to the temporary human dress. Even current prejudices in favor of males, nobly overcome in the New Testament, might be reflected in the choice of the Old Testament sign. The difference, then, is not theological at all but sociological. It belongs to the outward form and not to the inner matter of the divine revelation.

If, however, scripture is taken more seriously as God's word as well as man's, this account of the matter will hardly do. Some significance or purpose must be sought that stands materially related to the divine work signified by the signs. Along these lines the clue to a proper understanding of this particular distinction is to be found in the prophetic nature of the Old Testament sign in distinction from the apostolic nature of the New Testament sign. Circumcision, it will be recalled, was instituted along with the promise that blessing should come to all nations through Abraham's offspring. It thus points forward to the coming of the promised offspring and the shedding of the prefigured blood. As Paul points out, however, the one seed, while born of woman,[11] is the male seed.[12] Salvation was to come to both men and women through the divinely

[11]Galatians 4:4
[12]Galatians 3:16; cf. Isaiah 7:14; 9:6

ordained male, that is, the son of Abraham and the Son of God. One may thus see a peculiar aptness in the restriction of the anticipatory sign to the male, just as one may see a similar aptness in the extension of the backward-looking sign to both male and female now that all are one in the one seed and Savior.

This difference in administration is plain to see in the New Testament. Women were baptized, Lydia no less than Cornelius. In contrast, we look in vain for the suggested difference that whereas circumcision was given to the infants of covenant members, baptism is now to be reserved for those who can make a conscious decision and confession of faith. Appeal might be made to the baptism of Christ himself and the first subjects of Christian baptism. But this does not help. Christ and the first converts were, of course, baptized as adults. But these first baptisms in the New Testament are parallel to the first circumcision or circumcisions in the Old Testament. Abraham was circumcised as an adult. The Israelites were also circumcised as adults after the desert wanderings. When aliens were incorporated into the covenant people by conquest, purchase, or proselytizing, they too were circumcised as adults. But in each case the children of the household were also circumcised and then their children's children in each succeeding generation of faith. In view of the general correspondence and the absence of plain indications to the contrary, it is not unreasonable to conclude that the sign of the new covenant applies to children of the household as well as to adult converts. If the generation of primary evangelism is expanded to include both male and female converts, the generation of secondary evangelism is likewise expanded to include both male and female infants of covenant members receiving Christian upbringing and nurture.

2. We now come to the second reason why the continuity of circumcision and baptism is so important. The first, as we recall, is that in circumcision God deals with the family or people and not with the individual alone. The second is that circumcision is by its very nature and institution a sign of the covenant. At this point one must be on guard against a common misapprehension. Circumcision cannot be classified as part of the ceremonial law. In point of fact it was given long before the law if by the law we mean the Mosaic law. The paucity of reference to circumcision in the later codes of Exodus and Leviticus is indeed surprising. The law of circumcision came down from the time of Abraham, even though it fell into disuse during the period of bondage in Egypt. It was distinctly given to Abraham as the external "token" of the covenant that God made with him: "This is my covenant, which ye shall keep, between me and you and thy seed after thee; every man child among you shall be circumcised."[13] Circumcision, then, was more than a statute in the Mosaic legislation. It was significatory or sacramental in character—note the common sacramental identification of the sign and the thing signified. It had been established as a special sign at the very time when the covenant with Abraham was established, the covenant which underlay the separation of Israel as the progeny of Abraham and was fulfilled with the blessing that came on all people in Jesus Christ as his definitive offspring.

Now in the account of the institution of the covenant and of circumcision as its sign we are again in the world of thought which has already become familiar to us. In the first chapter, for example, we saw that the children of

[13]Genesis 17:10

22

believers, or even of one believer, are regarded as having a special status of holiness or separation. We have seen further that the two Old Testament types of baptism stand in a particular relationship to the divine covenant which is not with the individual in isolation but with the individual in a family or people. We now find that the covenant sign of circumcision is expressly connected with the divine election and calling not only of Abraham but also of "his seed after him in their generations." The covenant which it signifies is in fact an "everlasting covenant" and God engages to be God "unto thee and to thy seed after thee." This is why the sign is to be given not only to Abraham but to all the males of his household, young or old, and to all his male descendants as well, and even to the various aliens in different ways attached to him.

An apparent problem arises here. Has not the covenant God made with Abraham been abrogated by the new covenant that Christ instituted in his own blood? A casual reading of Hebrews suggests this but a more attentive study shows that the contrast in this Epistle is not between Abraham and Christ but between Moses and Christ. For the relation between Abraham and Christ we need to go to Romans 4. In this passage Paul tells us that there is a direct line between the covenant that God made with believing Abraham and the covenant that he established with those who are justified by faith in Jesus Christ.[14] Here, then, the relation is not one of antithesis but of fulfillment. Far from cancelling the covenant with Abraham and its promise, the covenant of the New Testament brings it to the inclusive fulfillment in which Abraham is the father not of Israel alone but of all believers.

---

[14]Romans 4:9–25; cf. Luke 1:55, 72–75

(In passing it might be noted that fulfillment as well as abrogation occurs in relation to the Mosaic covenant also.)

It is because the covenant has been fulfilled, not ended, that the prophetic or anticipatory sign is no longer applicable. Its place has been taken by the new sign of the fulfilled covenant, Christian baptism. The covenant itself remains—filled out, extended, yet unaltered in essential character and certainly not discarded. The promise is still "unto you, and to your children." It is also to as many as God shall call. New believers from the nations are added to the believing people of the old covenant in accordance with its promise. But there is no reason whatever to suppose that when these believers from the nations are added God changes course and begins to deal only with individuals in isolation. Indeed, the New Testament makes clear that this is not so. As in the case of Abraham the baptism of the household head is accompanied by the baptism of the entire household. If one spouse believes and the other does not, the believing partner sanctifies the unbeliever and the children are considered holy even if they cannot in every case be baptized. A nexus of believing arises in a family like that of Timothy.[15] With the fulfillment a difference has come in the form and scope of the covenant and the covenant sign has been altered. The covenant itself, however, is still the same eternal covenant, and the principle of divine election and operation has not changed.

In other words, when we study the Old Testament witness as it is explicitly and implicitly adduced in the New Testament, we find very strong support for the conclusions that were reached in the survey of New Testa-

[15] 2 Timothy 1:5

24

ment practice. In the events which prefigure baptism and in the sign which it replaces, the purpose and work of God are not with solitary individuals but with families and groups and the individuals within them. In each instance children are included in the promises of God along with their parents, so that they, too, are numbered among the covenant people. It is natural, then, that they should unquestioningly be included in the sign of the covenant, just as they participate in the events which are types of its fulfillment.

Obviously the key to the whole matter, as the Reformation churches have always insisted, is to be sought in the covenant and in its renewal and fulfillment in Jesus Christ. This means that our next step must be the very important one of asking whether we are right to interpret New Testament baptism as a sign of the fulfilled covenant, or whether, after all, it has some very different significance. This, perhaps, is the crux of the debate, unless one attempts the hazardous thesis that the Old Testament covenant has been completely outdated and the mode of God's operation altogether changed. For if baptism is not a sign of the covenant but of something else, then no compelling reason exists to apply it in the same way as the Old Testament sign and types. The New Testament may indeed force us to accept the fact that the one covenant is fulfilled and remains. The children of Christians may indeed enjoy covenant status. But if baptism is not a covenant sign, all this has no relevance to the question of its proper subjects. In spite of all the debates about the New Testament evidence and its proper exegesis, it is here if anywhere that the ways of those who baptize infants and those who do not diverge. But the divergence, as we shall see, is not merely in the doctrine and practice of baptism.

In relation to the meaning of baptism, it is a basic divergence in the understanding of all the ways and works of God. For this reason the baptismal issue needs to be weighed with special care and sobriety. It has more than the superficial significance that might easily be attached to it.

3
The Meaning
of Baptism

THE FACT OF BAPTISM and its general nature and administration do not give rise to any particular problems or disagreements. From the very first the disciples of Jesus clearly baptized in some form parallel to the baptism of John.[1] The risen Jesus, when giving them his final commission, told them to preach the gospel, to make disciples, and to baptize them into the name of the Father, the Son, and the Holy Spirit.[2] The apostles baptized the first converts on the day of Pentecost[3] and since then baptism has always been, with very few exceptions, the initiatory rite of discipleship. Baptism in the name of Christ is mentioned in Acts,[4] and although this has given rise to considerable discussion no significant deviation has been found in it. Through the centuries variations have also appeared with regard to the precise formula, mode, and especially

[1] John 4:1-2
[2] Matthew 28:19
[3] Acts 2:38, 41
[4] Cf. Acts 10:48; 19:5

the subjects of baptism. These variations have led to heated controversies; nevertheless, they have had little effect on the fact of baptism. For the most part—to accept the terminology of the Vincentian canon—baptism has been practiced in a valid and recognizable form always, everywhere, and by all.

If, however, we turn from the fact and the general character of baptism to its meaning and purpose, the matter is not so clear. On the one hand there have been those who invest the sacrament with an almost magical quality. For them the rite was divinely instituted as a means of entry both into the church and also into salvation. With the Holy Spirit, water serves as an agent of regeneration and of the infusion of virtues. If it is correctly administered and there are no impediments of insincerity, unbelief, or impenitence, as there can rarely be in infants, baptism is a guarantee, because it is an instrument, of internal cleansing, justification, and renewal. Hence the baptized person, at least at the moment of baptism, can be sure of eternal salvation. Equally, of course, the omission of baptism entails a serious risk, indeed the virtual certainty of eternal perdition except where omission is made good by the spiritual baptism of perfect conversion or the bloody baptism of martyrdom. On this view no problem of infant baptism arises. The significance of baptism lies in its instrumental function. The instrument is not meant for adults alone. To extend this necessary and efficacious instrument to all qualified infants is a simple act of obedience, service, and charity.

This is one view, but we need not spend unnecessary time on it. To be sure, a measure of real truth underlies it. Christ undoubtedly instituted baptism, and with the word and the Lord's Supper it may rightly be described as a means of grace. At least, many evangelical Christians accept this definition. Nevertheless, its interpretation as an almost automatic instrument for the infusing of grace finds little or no support either in the teaching and practice of the New Testament, or the anticipatory signs and types of the Old. The only possible verse which can be adduced for this understanding is John 3:5, and even if water is meant literally here the saying does not tell us anything about its mechanical functioning. In Acts, baptism is said to be for the remission of sins, but again nothing is said about its serving as an automatic instrument. The Epistles do not say a great deal about baptism. This is strange in any case but especially so if it was intended, and operated, as an indispensable agent of salvation. Paul, indeed, dismisses it in almost cavalier fashion in 1 Corinthians,[5] although his main point is that no importance ought to be attached to the human minister, as some misguided people apparently thought at Corinth. The Epistle to Titus again links baptism with regeneration,[6] but the particular mode of this relationship is not specified. 1 Peter, in contrast, seems to make it very plain that the external act does not in and of itself entail or effect the internal work.[7] It needs a good deal of speculative inference then, and a certain blindness to the general trend of biblical teaching, to derive this extreme understanding from the scriptures.

The opposite extreme seems at first to be much more convincing. The thesis here is that baptism serves, not as the instrument of something that is done for us, on us, or

---

[5] 1 Corinthians 1:13-17
[6] Titus 3:5
[7] 1 Peter 3:21

in us, but as a sign of something that we ourselves do. By this public act, in which we openly express our repentance from sin and profess our faith in Jesus Christ, we signify the turning away from the old life of sin and the entry into new life in Christ in whom we believe. The chief significance of the rite, then, is as an attestation of repentance and faith. Its purpose is to offer an opportunity for a public statement and, as it were, enactment of renunciation and renewal. From this standpoint it also has the significance of a test as the first step of Christian obedience. Similarly it can be viewed as a pledge or commitment to continuation in the life of discipleship now entered. If all this is true, then patently it makes no sense that baptism be given to infants. Whatever their covenant status, they cannot make a conscious personal decision or a personal confession of faith. Hence baptism as the enactment of such a decision and confession cannot have any meaning or serve any useful purpose for them. Indeed, when they grow older, it might even confuse them into thinking that a personal decision and confession are not demanded of them. Baptism, then, should be withheld until the time comes when, with their conversion and individual commitment, it can have proper significance and serve its true purpose.

It seems that various passages from scripture can be adduced in favor of this view of baptism as a confession of faith. Even in the Old Testament we find circumcision linked to faith. As Paul puts it, Abraham's circumcision was the seal of the righteousness of the faith he possessed while yet uncircumcised. When we look at Acts it is clear that adult converts made either a confession of faith or gave some sign of faith prior to their baptism. The Ethiopian eunuch provides an excellent example (except for the textual uncertainty of 8:37) when, in answer to Philip's challenge, he first testifies to his belief in Jesus as the Son of God and is then baptized. The very symbolism of the sacrament as vividly brought out by Paul in Romans 6 lays a certain stress on this aspect. Baptism is the believer's burial with Jesus and his subsequent rising again to the new life of the risen Lord. The truth in the association of baptism and faith has always been recognized by all churches. From the very first the baptismal liturgies found a place for the confession of faith as an essential part of the administration. Even when infants are baptized this element is not left out. The parents or sponsors must make a confession of faith either in their own names or vicariously in that of the child, which comes to much the same thing.

While all this is true and good, one must not leap hastily to the conclusion that it settles the matter. It is still worth investigating in the New Testament whether baptism is in fact constituted and administered solely or even primarily as an act or enactment of the personal faith and confession of the candidate. Where do we learn that this is the meaning and purpose of baptism? In what scripture do we read that when adult converts are baptized on confession of faith they are baptized in the first instance for this confession or as an active sign of their personal decision for Christ? Where do we find any reference to baptism as a first step of obedience or as a pledge of ongoing discipleship? No one will deny that a close and necessary connection exists, and ought to exist, between baptism and faith or baptism and confession. Where adult converts out of paganism are baptized, as in the primary evangelism of all the churches, it is necessary and right that baptism and personal faith go hand in hand. Where the children of professing Christians are baptized, it is no less necessary and right that a confession of faith be made, for the sign of the covenant is to be given only to those children belonging to the covenant in virtue of the confessed faith of their parent or parents. It is one thing, however, to say that the confession of faith must be included in baptism as an integral part of it. It is quite another to think or state that this confession constitutes the meaning and purpose of baptism.

When we investigate the matter in scripture we find that the situation is very different. In fact we ought to be warned at the outset by the very character of the baptismal sign. In contrast to the Lord's Supper it is an act in which the recipient has a passive, not an active role. Even an adult convert does not baptize as he takes, eats, or drinks. He is baptized. He does not do something for or to himself. Something is done for, to, and on him. When we turn to the relevant passages in scripture we find that this is not accidental, for baptism is not related primarily to what we do, to our faith, or to our decision or confession of faith, but to that which is done for us, to that on which our faith is set. In this again baptism corresponds to circumcision. Paul, as we have seen, undoubtedly links circumcision and faith, yet he does not call circumcision an enactment or expression of faith. He calls it a seal. Moreover, it is not strictly a seal of faith, but a seal of the righteousness of faith.[8] Nor is faith itself the righteousness. According to the whole argument of this first part of Romans righteousness is a gift and work of God reckoned on account of faith.[9] It is here that we begin to see the element of truth which unfortunately undergoes distortion in exaggerated sacramentalist and quasi-magical ideas of baptism.

[8]Romans 4:11
[9]Cf. Romans 3:24

In relation to baptism, surely the first thing to strike us is the emphasis placed not so much on the person baptized as on the one into whose name he or she is baptized. The words of institution in Matthew 28:19 tell us that baptism is to be into the name of the Father, the Son, and the Holy Spirit. In the Acts accounts we read of baptisms in the name of Jesus Christ, which implies the whole Trinity.[10] Paul disclaims the importance of the human minister only to enhance the one into whose name we are all baptized.[11] All this means that baptism does not primarily summon either ourselves or others to look at us and our faith and confession of faith. It invites both ourselves and others to look first at the one who is the object of our faith and whose gracious work we acknowledge when we confess our faith. To be sure, faith has an indispensable role. Nevertheless, salvation does not lie in our faith. Peter clearly proclaims that salvation lies in the name of Jesus Christ[12] and baptism, as a sign of the gospel like the Supper, was not instituted to witness to our own name as though we were the first thing. It was instituted to witness to the name and act of God into which we are caught up in faith. It is our baptism and confession of Christ only because it is Christ's baptizing and confession of us. Baptism finds its basic and central meaning as a sign and proclamation of the work of God whereby the righteousness of faith is sealed to us. It has only secondary and derivative meaning as the confession of our own faith and conversion.

It might be suggested, perhaps, that too much is being read into the mention of the Triune name (as if one could ever read in too much when God is mentioned). In reply

---

[10]E.g., Acts 2:38
[11]1 Corinthians 1:12–15
[12]Acts 4:12

to this possible objection we will look further in an attempt to see for and to what we are baptized when we are baptized into the name of the Father, Son, and Holy Spirit. Once again it quickly appears that in the New Testament the connection of baptism is not with what *we* do, with our conversion or confession, but with what *God* does for and in us in Jesus Christ and by the Holy Spirit, the forgiveness of sins and regeneration. In Acts 2:38, Peter urges those who are "cut to the heart" to repent and be baptized in the name of Christ for the remission of their sins. Similarly, when Ananias summons Paul to be baptized he is no doubt as concerned about his faith as Peter is about repentance; however, the accent falls elsewhere: "Arise, and be baptized, and wash away thy sins, calling on the name of the Lord."[13] Again in John 3:5, if the reference is indeed to water baptism, as seems likely enough, baptism is not linked at all to the believer's action but to regeneration through the ministry of the Holy Spirit. The same holds true in Titus 3:5 which establishes a parallel link between baptism and regeneration in the context of the life-giving work of the Holy Spirit.

Now it is evident that neither the forgiveness of sins nor regeneration is or can be a human work or even a human possibility. We can and must do certain things for ourselves within the totality of God's saving work. We are told to repent, call on the name of the Lord, believe, confess our faith, and receive forgiveness and renewal. We have to do these things if salvation is to be ours and we have to do them even if only enabled by virtue of what God does. Forgiveness and regeneration, however, are very plainly the work of God which we cannot and should

[13]Acts 22:16

not try to do. "Who can forgive sins but God only?"[14] The Pharisees were quite right when they put this accusing question before Jesus. They were wrong in failing to see that in Jesus they were dealing with God. Similarly the new birth is not of blood, nor of the will of man, nor of the will of the flesh, but of God.[15] If we are to be born again we must be born from above, born of the Spirit.[16] This means, however, that if baptism is primarily for remission and regeneration it does not focus on our necessary but secondary and derivative action, faith and the confession of faith. It focuses on the indispensable, primary, and originative action of God, the divine work of reconciliation and renewal. Baptism declares, signifies, and seals not what I do but what God has done, does, and will do for me.

The above is true even in the passage in Romans 6 which draws the inference of the believer's mortification and renewal. We will come back to this later. Yet we may note already that the central message of these verses, and that to which our baptism testifies, is the death, burial, and resurrection of Jesus Christ already enacted on our behalf. Only on this basis, in and with this work, is there even the possibility, let alone the reality, of our own death, burial, and rising again. The primary stress in this passage falls on the same point as in the other verses dealing with baptism. We are not just directed to ourselves and to our own faith and confession of faith or to our own dying to the old life and rising again to the new life. We are directed to God and to what God has done for us in

[14]Mark 2:7
[15]John 1:13
[16]John 3:3, 6

35

Jesus Christ, to what he does and will do for us and in us by the Holy Spirit. Only in this context and on this basis can we think of the necessary response of faith and of personal entry into God's reconciling and regenerating work.

Surely, then, we are forced to the conclusion that baptism is primarily a sign or seal of God's own work. Saying this, however, is simply another way of saying that it is a sign or seal of the covenant and its fulfillment in Jesus Christ. God's reconciling and regenerating work constitutes the fulfillment of the promise which lies at the heart of the covenant and of all God's dealings with his covenant people. From the very beginning the covenant carried with it the creation of a redeemed and renewed people, at first restricted in the main to a single nation but then broadened to embrace all nations. The fulfillment of the covenant in and with the death and resurrection of Jesus Christ means that the word of promise has been succeeded by the word of accomplishment, and the Old Testament signs of anticipation have been succeeded by the New Testament signs of recollection. If this is so, then it is no less perverse to treat baptism as the sign of personal faith than to treat circumcision as the sign of the faith of Abraham. Indeed, if this is possible, it is even more perverse. It is false to the New Testament and destroys the whole balance of the Christian gospel and the Christian life. It substitutes an anthropocentric meaning for the theocentric meaning. It puts the "I" and its decision in the place of God and his decision. It gives the primacy and honor to man and his work and not as it should to God and his work. It gives this work of man an apparent importance of its own in independence of Jesus Christ and the atonement and the Holy Spirit and regeneration. It finds the critical point in our turning to God rather than his turning to us and his turning us to himself. In other words, it turns the gospel upside down. In so doing it misses the real meaning and purpose of the gospel ordinance or sacrament.

By its very nature baptism is calculated to drive home the personal application of the divine work. The same was true of circumcision. Like circumcision, however, it does so only as it proclaims the divine work which is the work of the covenant fulfilled in Jesus Christ by the Holy Spirit. In the chapters that follow we will examine this proclamation more closely in relation to God's covenant work and the three persons of the Triune Godhead into whose name we are baptized.

4
The Election of the Father

Baptism into the name of God the Father declares to us the supreme fact that God has a purpose of love for us.[1] God is the author of our life. This in itself must be considered an expression of his wise, strong, and gracious choice. God is also the ruler of our life. Here again, in view of the complexity which has been introduced by our disobedience, evidence is given of the sovereignty of his grace. But this is not the end of the matter. The God of creation and providence is also the author of our salvation. He willed and planned it from all eternity.[2] In Christ he elected us to be covenant-partners with himself, that he should be our God and we should be his people.[3] He loved us long before we could ever love him.[4] When we proved unworthy of his love, defying him, breaking his

[1]Cf. John 3:16
[2]Cf. Ephesians 1:3–4
[3]Cf. 1 Peter 2:9
[4]1 John 4:10

commandment, and disrupting the fellowship which he had established, he did not abandon his purpose of grace. He did not change his primary and basic plan, but carried through his original intention of love in the history of salvation which begins with the promise of Eden,[5] takes shape in the call of Abraham and the deliverance of Israel out of Egypt, culminates in the coming of Jesus as Son of Man and Son of God, and will be consummated in his coming again and his kingdom. As the sign and seal of the covenant and its fulfillment, baptism into the Triune name points us to this electing grace of the Father.

Now it cannot be insisted too strongly or too often that in the election and the covenant the initiative rests entirely and exclusively with God. "It is not of him that willeth, nor of him that runneth, but of God that sheweth mercy."[6] Grace is rightly described as free or sovereign. Election rests on no merit, claim, or act of man. That there is a covenant at all is not due to any desire, desert, or deed of our own. It is due wholly and utterly to the fact that in free grace God willed to enter into covenant and thus set up the covenant himself. Man could not decide to be created and could not create himself. Sinful man could not choose and effect the working out of his acts for his own good and not for evil. Fallen man could not elect to enter into fellowship with God and then establish that fellowship. Dying man could not decide to have a new life nor could he give himself a new life. Nor was God under any extrinsic necessity or obligation to create the human race, to sustain it, and when it fell away from him to restore it. He elected to do these things on his own initia-

[5]Genesis 3:15
[6]Romans 9:16

tive and did so out of unmerited love. Having thus elected to do them, he did them in his own wisdom, grace, and power. Election implies the absolute primacy of God.

This is finely illustrated in the story of Abraham which is so important in relation to the covenant. The beginning of the dealings between God and Abraham was not due to Abraham's seeking after God. Abraham possibly engaged in a religious quest—he would be neither the first nor the last to do so. But we can only speculate here; the biblical record tells us nothing about it. The possibility has in itself no importance. What counts first and foremost is God's calling of Abraham.[7] Abraham did not decide that it would be a good idea if he were to move out of Ur, acquire a new religion, and become the father of a new people—God decided. God summoned him to the land of promise. God gave him the covenant and its promise. God in grace elected Abraham. All that followed by way of faith, obedience, hope, worship, and service on Abraham's part was simply the result of this election. If Abraham also elected God, he did so only because God first elected him.

The same truth emerges when we consider the position of Israel as the chosen people or the people of the covenant. The whole point of this is that Israel is not chosen because of any intrinsic qualifications. Its own prophets, not prejudiced anti-Semites, tell us that it had no distinction among the nations, not even that of a supposed national genius for religion, let alone numerical size, political or economic power, or highly developed culture.[8] Candidly, if hyperbolically, the Old Testament says that in some ways it was the most insignificant of all

[7]Genesis 12:1
[8]Ezekiel 16:3-5

40

peoples,[9] at least at the time when God elected it. It was for this very reason that God chose Israel, named it by his own name, separated it from the nations, and established his covenant with it. He made it explicit that no human qualifications could influence his choice by deliberately setting aside the nations seeming to be the most imposing and electing the one with nothing of its own to advance. The divine initiative of grace could hardly be presented more clearly than in this central fact of the Old Testament history and message.

The same gracious initiative may be seen in God's dealings with individuals within the family of Abraham. God does not accept as the child of promise the son whom Abraham sires in an unfortunate effort to do God's work for him.[10] He then sets aside the right of primogeniture when it comes to Esau and Jacob.[11] Even religion does not count as a reason for election, for of all the sons of Jacob, Joseph most clearly bears the mark of divine favor yet at the end of the day the tribal election surprisingly falls on Judah.[12] Significantly, indeed, women of different nationalities like Ruth and dubious morality like Bathsheba are chosen in the outworking of the divine purpose and can thus find a place in the genealogy of Christ.[13] As Mary so eloquently put it, the freedom of the divine election meant the removal of the high and mighty from their seats and the exalting of the poor and meek.[14]

The New Testament not only offers further illustra-

[9]Cf. Deuteronomy 7:7
[10]Genesis 16
[11]Genesis 25:23
[12]Genesis 49:10
[13]Matthew 1:5–6
[14]Luke 1:52

tion of this sovereignty of electing grace, but also formulates it in many different ways. The Lord plainly tells his disciples that they have not chosen him but he has chosen them.[15] The record leaves us in no doubt that this election was not on the basis of aptitude, achievement, merit, or desire. Again, Paul emphasizes the graciousness of the divine calling and its incompatibility with all human ideas when he warns the Corinthians: "For ye see your calling, brethren. . . ."[16] In Ephesians, too, believers are referred back to their eternal election in Jesus Christ: "According as he hath chosen us in him before the foundation of the world."[17] This time baptism itself is fairly clearly linked with the calling, for the passage goes on to say that "after that ye believed [this is written in the first instance to adult converts], ye were sealed with that Holy Spirit of promise, which is the earnest of our inheritance until the redemption of the purchased possession."[18] The point could hardly be made more clearly or firmly. The event which is signified and sealed by the Spirit in baptism does not begin with an individual human decision. It begins with the divine decision of covenant election.

A covenant, of course, is twofold. Hence a place is naturally left for human response. Indeed, the covenant, which is no mere bargain or contract, demands and elicits this response. If God elects to be the God of Abraham, Israel, the church, or individual Christians, then Abraham, Israel, the church, and individual Christians are to be the people of God. This aspect is also brought out in baptism inasmuch as a confession of faith is made and

15John 15:16
161 Corinthians 1:26-28
17Ephesians 1:4
18Ephesians 1:13-14

there is thus an entry into the work of God and an accep-
tance of the instituted covenant relationship with God. It
is to be noted, however, that since the covenant is not a
mutual arrangement, the human decision is incontestably
secondary and derivative. This does not mean that it is
unimportant or unnecessary nor that we may despise, disparage, or virtually eliminate it. Indeed, the very fact that
it is secondary and derivative gives to the human election
of God its true validity, reality, and honor. God calls the
disciple, and in virtue of this call the disciple may and
must rise up and follow. He cannot decide to follow before
he is called. He cannot offer terms to God or propose a
contractual or covenantal relation from his side. He can be
authentically in covenant only because God has first put
him in covenant. He can be saved only because God first
willed and achieved salvation for him. The electing of
God the Father has clear precedence over the electing of
man the son. The decision of man for God presupposes
the prior decision of God for man.

   An important implication of this biblical truth may be
briefly noted here. If baptism points us first and chiefly to
the divine election, the absence of the human decision
does not have to destroy the meaning of the sacrament or
render its administration futile. In some cases this will
obviously be true. When a person knowingly rejects the
divine call to faith and discipleship, denying the divine
election and refusing to enter into covenant relationship,
there can be no question of baptism, not even on the plea
that it might serve as a testimony to the divine will for this
person. But this is not such a live issue today as it might
have been in times of more widespread conventional
Christianity, for in the majority of instances of this kind
baptism will not be desired. With the children of confess-

ing Christians, however, as with the descendants of Abraham, we have a very different situation. For if baptism is now administered before the time has come for the human decision which must follow and be grounded in the divine choice, the result is singularly to magnify the divine initiative of grace which is the primary message of the ordinance. The sacrament serves as a sign and seal of God's election and calling to which the right response, looked for in due time, is man's faith and penitence. The reformers grasped this point well when they pointed out that if faith is the prerequisite of baptism in the case of adult converts, in that of the children of professed believers the proper prerequisite is divine calling or election.

Can we be sure, however, that the election of the Father does extend to the children of believers along with the parents? Are such children called, not merely in the sense that God wills the salvation of all or that Christ offered himself for all, but in a more specific way? We have already referred to certain passages in the New Testament which strikingly suggest this is so. These are confirmed by the Old Testament types to which the New Testament points, and more especially by the Old Testament sign of the covenant which baptism has obviously replaced. The general witness of the Old Testament provides additional confirmation, for it shows us that although individual repentance and faith are consistently required,[19] God does not deal with individuals in isolation but with individuals in families, peoples, and generations.[20] In the Old Testament, of course, this involved a certain exclusiveness, for apart from aliens who attached

[19]Cf. Romans 2:28–29
[20]Genesis 17:7–8

themselves to Israel, the divine election centered particularly upon one people.[21] But the exclusiveness was for the sake of an ultimate comprehensiveness in and through the promised seed to which the whole history of Israel pointed and moved.[22] Today God's purpose is for all nations and peoples, "even as many as the Lord our God shall call."[23] God has not set his name on one nation alone, but in every race, tribe, kindred, tongue, and people. Wherever the gospel is preached—and it is to be preached to everyone[24]—men and women may enter into the covenant of grace which God has purposed for them according to his own free and unchanging election and promise. We have no reason to suppose, however, that when they do so the covenant then deals only with the individuals concerned and has no application to their families in succeeding generations. Scripture does not tell us there has been this crucial change in God's covenant dealings. The evidence points the other way. God does not give with one hand, extending the covenant in space, only to take away with the other, restricting the covenant in time. Surely the covenant of God fulfilled in Jesus Christ still remains to a thousand generations when the gospel is preached and received, so that the children of confessing Christians awaken to self-conscious life with the promise of the gospel in their ears and may thus have the mark of the covenant on their bodies. For them, as for the children of Old Testament Israel, election constitutes a posited reality. The call to them is not to enter into a totally new covenant relationship proclaimed for the first time from outside. It

[21]Cf. Amos 3:2
[22]Genesis 17:4; Isaiah 49:6
[23]Acts 2:39
[24]Matthew 28:19

is to enter personally into the covenant relationship of which they already have both the promise and the sign or seal in virtue of their Christian descent.

Here, however, a difficulty arises. Not all the children of confessing Christians do in fact take up their covenant membership in personal repentance and faith in Jesus Christ. Indeed, far too many do not, and never can anyone be sure that specific individuals will. Until it is known, then, whether they have done so, is it not rash and possibly misleading to include them within the divine election and covenant and to bring them under its sign? Will not talk and action of this kind either presuppose a divine election irrespective of human rejection or else rob the divine election of any ultimate reality or relevance?

The difficulty may be eased in two ways. First, the example of Old Testament Israel should again be considered. To all Israel, as Paul puts it, belonged "the adoption, and the glory, and the covenants, and the giving of the law, and the service of God, and the promises."[25] Nevertheless, if we study the different generations of Israelites, we find that always many apostates existed side by side with genuine believers in God. The proportion obviously varied in different periods. Times of reformation alternated with times of large-scale licentiousness and idolatry. In Elijah's day there were in the northern kingdom no more than seven thousand who had not bowed the knee to Baal,[26] and even this was more than the prophet himself had supposed.[27] In spite of this, however, Israel still remained the people of the covenant. A remnant was preserved even when the situation became so bad that a

[25]Romans 9:4
[26]1 Kings 19:18
[27]1 Kings 19:14

majority of the people was cast off by God and ejected from the land of promise.[28] This was especially true in Judah, where the covenant sign of circumcision survived the exile and the people could still be properly described as the covenant people in spite of the judgment of God which came upon them. The unfaithfulness of one part of a generation, or even of virtually a whole generation, could not defeat the indefatigable and gracious faithfulness of God in his fatherly election.

Secondly, the difficulty arises on any understanding of baptism. Even when baptism is viewed as an automatically efficacious instrument of grace, its work may still be undone by subsequent unbelief or other mortal sin. Similarly, when baptism is given only after very careful screening and what is thought to be a credible confession of faith, no guarantee exists that a genuine conversion has taken place and thus lies behind the external profession. It is all very well to keep talking about believers' baptism—an excellent slogan—but since God alone knows the heart,[29] who are we to say for sure that baptism is ever more than confessors' baptism? Who can know that those who are baptized on confession of faith do in reality enter into the covenant relation with God, enjoy the remission of sins, and receive new life by the regenerative activity of the Holy Spirit? The New Testament itself issues an unmistakable warning here. Simon Magus received adult baptism on what seemed to be a sincere profession of faith; nevertheless, his subsequent denunciation by Peter showed that the inner reality differed widely from the outward expression.[30]

---

[28] 2 Kings 17; 2 Chronicles 30:11
[29] 1 Samuel 16:7
[30] Acts 8:13–24

No matter how baptism is understood, water baptism can never be equated directly with the divine election of individuals which will be disclosed and known, not on the day of church admission, but on the day of judgment. Water baptism can be equated directly only with that external calling, election, or covenant membership known either by an adult profession of faith, a Christian descent, or, as some would think, the sacramental administration itself. Scripture clearly asserts that corporately God's covenant is with the company of those who profess his name and descend from professing parents. This is the company which, as the object of divine grace, is the elect or chosen people, the church. To this company, then, belongs by divinely given right the sign or seal of the covenant. Whether or not beyond that there is in a given case the individual election which implies the electing of God in personal repentance and faith is another matter. No one has any means of knowing this and it therefore can never serve as a norm in baptismal administration.

In this connection it is worth noting that some who will not practice infant baptism hold the pathetic, rather impudent, as well as imprudent view that they can anticipate the final judgment, discern the secrets of the heart, and thus separate true believers from hypocrites or purely nominal Christians. Sometimes, like Elijah, they are led in this way to despair of almost all their fellow-confessors, so that they only are left. They may or may not be right. But they are taking a rash step if on the ground of their own judgment they refuse the covenant sign to those who share the corporate election and thus qualify for its sign either by confession or descent. The disciples learned this when they thought that Jesus could not possibly be interested in certain groups of people and when they apparently concluded that children could not be received by him or be the recipients of his gracious blessing. This attitude presupposes a fancied ability to do what God alone can do, namely, make an inner judgment. It also presupposes an imagined knowledge of what God is doing or will do in a specific life at a specific time or place. In other words, it does not take seriously enough the election of the Father where all else has its origin. "I will be gracious to whom I will be gracious"[31] is a saying which must never be forgotten or obscured when the redemptive dealings of God are at issue. The beginning always lies in the Father's gracious, merciful, and unmerited election. In baptism, testimony is borne to this election as the sacrament is given to all those who outwardly are called by his name, whether by their own confession or that of their fathers and forefathers. God himself taught us in scripture that there should be this testimony. When he chooses that his name should be set in a family, society, or church, it is not for any person, let alone his disciples, to attempt to hold back this testimony on the ground that external confession is unsupported by internal faith. Only when a family, society, or church deliberately and finally rejects God's divine purpose of grace should the testimony cease, but then there will no longer be any desire for or possibility of it, so that it will tend to die away of itself, as infant baptism has diminished in many secularized communities today.

Since baptism as the sign of the covenant takes us back to the beginning of salvation in the eternal and gracious purpose of God, it is right and proper that in it the stress should fall not on the human election of faith but on the

[31]Exodus 33:19

divine election of grace preceding it. In cases of adult converts from paganism, the holding out of the covenant promises and the individual fulfilling of the divine purpose will be more or less coincident with the decision of faith and entry into the covenant people. Even here, however, baptism should be given and proclaimed as a reaffirmation of the gracious will of God rather than an expression or enactment of faith. When the infants of confessing Christians are baptized, these come under the divine promises and share in the corporate election from the very beginning. They grow up in the sphere of the divine calling and the related prayer and proclamation and teaching of the holy people. There never is a time when the electing purpose of God is not held out over them and to them. Hence the decision of faith, the electing of God in which God's individual electing comes to personal fulfillment, is evoked as they come to know the divine purpose which is declared by the word taught them and the sign set over them. Whether administered to adult converts or Christian children, baptism has the common function of directing us to the gracious electing will of the Father which determined our salvation not only before our baptism but also before all creation—a will shown to be for us by the fact that the gospel has now reached out to us or by the fact that we are born into an existing sphere of its operation.

There is just one final point and this leads us on to the next chapter. The eternal election of the Father is linked to the preaching of the gospel. This is so because the gracious purpose of God has been fulfilled in the reconciling work which the gospel proclaims. When we are baptized, then, we are baptized into a purpose already accomplished. Baptism does not bear witness to a salvation brought into being only when I myself believe. It bears witness to a salvation which God brought into being when he acted for us in fulfillment of his election of grace. The purposes and promises of God are held out to us as promises and purposes already fulfilled in this way. The baptism of both adults and infants points us not only to the eternal election of the Father but also to the historical enactment of this election which took place, as scripture tells us, in Jesus Christ. To see how this is so and what it implies we must now move from the eternal election of the Father to its accomplishment in the once-for-all reconciliation of the Son.

5
The Reconciliation
of the Son

BAPTISM into the name of God the Son declares to us the supreme fact that God has indeed fulfilled his purpose of grace for us and implemented the election, the covenant, and the promises. This is perhaps the real explanation of the apostolic administration of baptism in the name of Jesus Christ alone, for the whole point of the apostolic message is that God has acted decisively and definitively for us in Jesus Christ.[1] Reconciliation has now been made. It can now be declared and accepted in him. The name of Jesus Christ, of course, carries with it the whole Trinity. Baptism can never be into three names, only one. It was to accomplish the will of the Father who sent him that Jesus Christ came.[2] It was in the power of the Holy Spirit, of whom he was conceived, that he taught, acted, died, and rose again.[3] Nevertheless, the name of Jesus Christ is central and crucial, because it is in him and his work that

[1]Hebrews 1:1–3
[2]John 4:34; Hebrews 10:9
[3]Luke 1:35; Matthew 12:28, etc.

the divine purpose has been brought to its accomplishment.

The same point is reached in another way when we recall that baptism is connected with the remission of sins. Sin constitutes the obstacle to covenant fellowship with God. A breach was made in the original relation to God when man fell into sin. Sin, therefore, cuts across the divine purpose and seems to make impossible the Father's election. If this election is to stand, if God's original purpose is still to be attained, if there is to be a covenant between God and the creature that has fallen away from and sinned against him, sin must in some way be overcome. It means, in effect, that sin must be forgiven and its consequences arrested. Man himself, of course, cannot forgive his own sin. Nor can he earn forgiveness by making retribution. In these circumstances God might easily and justly have abandoned the sinner to destruction, especially as no evident alternative seemed to present itself. But this, as we have seen, would have meant the negation of his own gracious purpose in election and the overthrow of his covenant. Hence a new initiative was exercised. Jesus, the divine Son, came into the world to make expiation, to bring forgiveness, to effect reconciliation, to deal with sin, and thereby to implement the covenant and fulfill the election. He was given the name of Jesus because he was to save his people from their sins.[4] He declared both his authority and his mission by uttering the divine word of forgiveness.[5] Finally he gave his life a ransom for many,[6] for although forgiveness may be free in the sense that it is free to us, that we have neither to earn

[4]Matthew 1:21
[5]Matthew 9:2
[6]Mark 10:45

nor buy it, this does not mean that it is without cost to God. The apostles went out into the world after the atoning death and the life-giving resurrection of Jesus knowing that reconciliation had been effected and declaring the remission of sins in the name of Jesus.[7]

It must be emphasized that the remission of sins and the implementing of the divine election in him does not involve merely the coming of Christ but also his sacrificial death. The incarnation, of course, is an integral part of the divine self-giving in the Son. So is the ministry of word and work. The life of Christ must not be isolated from his death. Nevertheless, the movement of self-sacrificial abasement on behalf of sinners reaches its climax only with his passion and death. If baptism is associated with the remission of sins, it is specifically associated with the vicarious death which is the final declaration of Christ's self-sacrifice and the base for divine forgiveness.

We can think of this vicarious work in many ways. In the language of cultic sacrifice, for example, we can say with Hebrews that without the shedding of blood there is no remission.[8] We might also remember that the Old Testament sign of circumcision pointed forward to the shed blood of the promised son. Or we can adopt the more legal language of Paul and speak of the representative or substitutionary bearing of the judgment of sin. When we are baptized into Jesus Christ we are baptized into his death for us.[9] This vicarious death of Christ in which he took our sin upon himself is the way in which God could and did fulfill his eternal purpose of election in face of the obstacle

[7]Acts 5:31
[8]Hebrews 9:22
[9]Romans 6:3–4

of human sin. For sin had to be removed and destroyed. Inevitably, it seemed, the destruction of sin would entail the destruction of the sinner. But Christ incarnate, the sinless Son, accepted the destruction representatively for all others, in their place, and on their behalf, that they might be destroyed as sinners in him, not in themselves, and at the same time be raised up again with him as new and righteous people.

Thus baptism, in which we are first reminded of the death-dealing power of water, is baptism into the death of Christ, because in that death sin is destroyed and the sinner is vicariously destroyed. Yet the destruction of the sinner in Christ is with a view to his rising again, not as the old sinner, but as a new and righteous man in Christ. Baptism, in which we also recall the life-giving power of water, is baptism into the vicarious resurrection of Christ as well. For in that resurrection those who died in Christ are representatively raised in him to newness of life. Because the final purpose of God is not destruction but renewal and new creation, baptism is linked not merely with the judgment on sin but also with its remission, the removal of sin from the sinner, and the replacement of the sinner by the saint who can stand before God's judgment and begin the life of righteousness and love. This will also lead to the further significance of baptism as regeneration and ultimately the resurrection from the dead.

From all this it may be seen how intimately the baptism for remission of sins is related to the death and resurrection of Christ, and especially to his death where the accent seems to be placed. This relationship is not just suggested by the imagery, for according to the scriptural records God deliberately selected and instituted the sign so that the imagery would portray the reality. Nor is it merely a projection back from the individual baptismal experience of death to sin and regeneration to righteousness. Indeed, when we turn to the gospels we discover that the very reverse is the case. The death and resurrection of Christ are the true baptism of which our own baptism and baptismal experience are but a likeness, reflection, or, in a strictly qualified sense, repetition. In this respect baptism resembles the Lord's Supper, for there, too, the outpoured blood of Christ on the cross is the true and proper cup to which our sacramental cup bears witness.[10] To say this is not to indulge in fanciful theologizing. Jesus states the matter clearly when he says in reference to baptism: "I have a baptism to be baptized with; and how am I straitened till it be accomplished!"[11] In reference to the cup he says: "This cup is the new testament in my blood, which is shed for you,"[12] and later he prays in Gethsemane: "Father, if thou be willing, remove this cup from me."[13] He brings the two together in the challenge to the sons of Zebedee: "Are ye able to drink of the cup that I shall drink of, and to be baptized with the baptism that I am baptized with?"[14] In all these cases there is no doubt that in both the words and the mind of Jesus the reference is to his approaching death on the cross. The death of Jesus, followed at once by his rising again, is thus the true baptism or the true cup. Every subsequent cup or baptism is primarily a witness to the vicarious death and resurrection of Christ.

But now we must try to pin down in greater detail the

[10] 1 Corinthians 11:26
[11] Luke 12:50
[12] Luke 22:20
[13] Luke 22:42
[14] Matthew 20:22

meaning of the baptism of Christ's death and in what sense it fulfills the eternal purpose of God in election also declared in the baptismal ordinance. Appropriately enough, Christ's own baptism in the River Jordan gives us the right clue. It was just as strange, if less drastic, that Jesus should be baptized by John as that he should be baptized in his own blood on Golgotha. For John's baptism was a baptism of penitent sinners[15] and, as John himself realized, Jesus was not a sinner. Why then, in spite of the Baptist's protest, should Jesus not only accept baptism but insist on it? Various reasons can be given, but even if we take the common view that it signifies the entrance of Jesus on his public ministry, it finally seems to indicate the following. There in the River Jordan, at the inauguration of his ministry, Jesus gave himself up to a saving identification with sinners. He did this first of all in the baptism of repentance. In this way he directly entered a ministry of substitutionary or vicarious representation. In so doing he was at once endorsed by the Father and empowered by the Holy Spirit. But he was also exposed to all the crafts and assaults of the devil in a futile attempt to entice him off this path to a more immediately attractive and apparently more promising way. At the end of the road, on the cross of Golgotha, he was ready to go even further on the same path in spite of the final temptation of Gethsemane. For there, in his true and final baptism, he accepted all the sins of mankind and all the consequences of those sins, and by doing so alone became the representative substitute of sinners, taking their place, becoming their sin, and dying their death. Thus, in him sinners might die yet also be raised again to a new life freed from

[15]Matthew 3:6

sin and might enjoy the covenant fellowship which God from all eternity designed and purposed for them. Paul sums it all up in the pregnant sentence: "For he hath made him to be sin for us, who knew no sin; that we might be made the righteousness of God in him."[16]

Now in our baptism it is quite true that we declare our own dying and rising again with Christ. Baptism speaks to us of a responsive identification with Christ, of a personal entry into his vicarious death and resurrection. It is necessary that there be this dying and rising again in repentence as the renunciation of the old life and in faith as the turning to the new. Nevertheless, this personal death and resurrection through identification with Christ is not in itself of primary importance. The first thing, and that to which baptism directs us initially, is the dying and rising again of Christ in identification with us and on our behalf. It is an unfortunate reversal of the gospel message, or at least of the gospel emphasis, if in baptism we allow our own dying and rising again to occupy center stage and push the dying and rising again of Christ out into the wings. We are not to think that ours is the real baptism, and then apply the term in a transferred or figurative sense to the reconciling work of the Son. The truth is that the reconciling work of the Son is the original baptism and our own dying and rising again with Christ is the copy and reflection. The proper baptism declared in every baptism is the vicarious dying and rising again of Christ in which expiation is made for sin, reconciliation is effected, new life is inaugurated, the covenant of God with man is restored, the election of the Father is fulfilled, and the divine purpose of grace is thus realized in spite of man's sin and fall.

[16]2 Corinthians 5:21

Why is it so necessary that we insist on this emphasis? Because it alone can keep before us the fact that Christ's death and resurrection are vicarious, substitutionary, and representative. This means that they are in all literalness a death and resurrection for us; indeed, they are our own death and resurrection. It is only in this death and resurrection, not in an independent one of our own, that we can be forgiven, reconciled, accepted, renewed, and finally redeemed in the sense of Romans 8:23. It is only in and by virtue of this death and resurrection that we ourselves can die and rise again, which we do when we enter into the death and resurrection of Christ for us by repentance and faith. Our repentance and faith are not the real baptism; it is the vicarious or representative dying and rising again of Christ in and by which all sinners died and were raised again some two thousand years ago at Calvary. The trouble with so many of us is that we talk very easily about representation or substitution or even justification without being aware of the tremendous reality and sweep of it in the New Testament. Paul speaks boldly: "Because we thus judge, that if one died for all, then were all dead";[17] or again: "For ye are dead, and your life is hid with Christ in God";[18] or again: "For if through the offence of one many be dead, much more the grace of God, and the gift by grace, which is by one man, Jesus Christ, hath abounded unto many."[19] The witness of John is similar, for in the Gospel we read that the believer in Christ "shall not come into condemnation, but is passed from death unto life."[20] This does not mean, of course, that the be-

[17] 2 Corinthians 5:14
[18] Colossians 3:3
[19] Romans 5:15
[20] John 5:24

liever has as yet been literally raised again. On the other hand, it seems to be much more than a reference to the awakening of faith. In the general context of John regeneration is no doubt in view. The new birth, however, is related to the fact that the believer is already dead and risen again in the vicarious death and resurrection which Jesus Christ has already undergone in our place and on our behalf.

If this is so, however, the primary and proper reference of baptism is not to a present event in us but to a past event for us. Here we have the real *opus operatum* or finished work[21] of baptism—an authentic historical work, not the poetical or mythical representation of a subjective phenomenon. In our baptism we have an affirmation of the message of the gospel that Christ's death and resurrection were not for himself but for us. They were so literally for us that in Christ our old life is not simply pardoned; it is dead and done with. The judgment of God has already been passed and executed on it. It is gone forever and will never again be remembered. Yet this does not mean our eternal loss, for in Christ a new life has taken over. Christ is risen, and we too are raised to newness of life in him. In this new life we can be presented faultless before God[22] and live and reign with Christ to all eternity.[23] As far as our lives here on earth are concerned, we do not yet see this. "We walk by faith, not by sight."[24] But we know that it is so, for we see Jesus who died and rose again, and we realize that he died and rose again as our substitute and representative. It has taken place already because it has taken place in him, and in him for us.

[21]John 19:30
[22]Jude 24
[23]Romans 8:17
[24]2 Corinthians 5:7

Every baptism, therefore, proclaims the gospel of reconciliation by pointing us back to the vicarious act in which all believers, and in a sense all men in general, died and rose again already in Jesus Christ. When this is understood, the adult confessor will not say: "By my repentance and faith I have died and risen again and to this I bear witness in my baptism." Instead he will say: "Jesus Christ has died and risen again in my place, and entering into that death and resurrection I bear witness to it in my baptism, and thank him for it." Similarly the Christian parent will not say: "I bring my child to baptism because it will accomplish his death and resurrection." Nor will he say: "My child cannot die and rise again until he or she comes to repentance and faith, and therefore it would be pointless to bring this child to the sign of death and resurrection." Instead he will say: "My child has died and risen again already in Jesus Christ his representative and substitute, and therefore I will have him or her marked with the sign of vicarious death and resurrection as a confirmation of it and also as a direction to enter into it, when the time comes, in personal repentance and faith."

Of course there is a danger here as with every *opus operatum*. If Jesus Christ did in fact die and rise again for us, one might argue, what does it matter whether we believe or not? Do we need to do more than simply note the fact and then pass on the news to others? What sense can it make to come to a decision of our own and to appeal to others to do so? When news of some event reaches us, nothing we can think or say or do can alter the reality and validity of what has already taken place. If, then, we have to take seriously the vicarious aspect of Christ's work—so seriously that dying and rising again are already done for us in him—then surely this seems to carry with it a final obliteration of personal decision.

That this danger is not imaginary is shown by a recent tendency in many theological circles radically to reinterpret evangelism as a mere announcement of the good news that all are renewed and reconciled in Christ. Along these lines infant baptism makes excellent sense but it also increases the danger. The very objectivity or factuality of salvation to which it bears witness becomes a liability instead of an asset. Infants, it might be thought, are baptized into a salvation already achieved and thus when they grow older need do no more about it. The only obligation that exists is that of informing them later what baptism is all about. No responsive identification with Christ in personal death and resurrection need be asked for, since none is required.

If the danger at this extreme is obvious, one should not forget that the danger at the other extreme is no less serious. In this case all the emphasis is put on the personal dying and rising again in faith, so that the vicarious work of Christ is either obscured or replaced. When this happens the personal dying and rising again loses its point. For what meaning can my death and resurrection have except on the basis of Christ's? How can I even accomplish it apart from him? Whether I like it or not, the fact remains that Christ's vicarious work is genuinely vicarious. Christ has taken my place and acted for me. If he had not, I could only die in my sins and be raised to eternal judgment. Since he has, however, I cannot attempt a dying and rising again of my own with that of Christ merely as a model or symbol. Henceforth I must either find my true self in Christ or have no place to go and be finally and utterly lost. Without Christ any supposed dying and rising again of mine can be only an illusion. There is no place for me except in Jesus Christ who has taken my place.

It may be noted that when this aspect of the baptismal

message is properly grasped, the truth of the finished work of Christ does not leave any room for complacency or inactivity. If it has all the assurance it also has all the exclusiveness of that which is done. Christ has in fact identified himself with us and acted for us. Therefore, this is our only possibility, we now have to identify ourselves with him and participate in his act for us. If we still think that, notwithstanding Christ's work, our salvation lies in the self-identification of us with him, we run a dreadful risk of delusion and distortion. If, on the other hand, we treat the fact with indifference or reject it altogether, we cannot alter its truth but, trying to live apart from it, we can exclude ourselves from its truth and therewith from its redemptive benefits.

These two points cannot be separated. Self-identification with Christ is demanded. Without it the self is divorced from the fact of Christ's substitutionary representation. As Paul put it, God was in Christ reconciling the world to himself and for this very reason the appeal must be made that we are to be reconciled to God.[25] Yet self-identification with Christ is the appeal of the gospel and not the saving act constituting the message. The saving act is Christ himself in his vicarious life, death, and resurrection. It is an accomplished act apart from our necessary response to it. It is not our being reconciled to God, although this is implied and included, but God's reconciling of us to himself. As Jesus so simply stated: It is finished. Nothing that we can do can add to or replace this finished work. We can only accept it in the responsive movement of the death of the old self and the rising again of the new.

A chief value of infant baptism is that it is so well

[25] 2 Corinthians 5:19–20

calculated to keep before us this essential and central element in the work of God and the gospel. The very helplessness of infants underscores the truth that God's salvation is accomplished vicariously for us, that we can neither achieve, supplement, complement, nor complete it, that we must never try to dispute with Christ the place that he has taken for us. Adult baptism, of course, maintains the balance. If the temptation in adult baptism is to lay too much stress on the human movement, the temptation in infant baptism is to lay too little stress on it and thereby to destroy the evangelistic bearing of the news of God's saving action. We certainly have to tell people first that Christ has died and risen again for us and that salvation lies in this vicarious act alone. Having done this, however, we have also to urge people to die with Christ to sin and to rise again with him in righteousness on the basis and in the strength of that primary death and resurrection. This personal application of the gospel brings us into the distinctive sphere of the Holy Spirit and the ministry of the Holy Spirit. It is, therefore, in relation to the particular function and activity of the Spirit that we must now turn.

6
The Regeneration
of the Spirit

Baptism into the name of the Holy Spirit declares to us the supreme fact that the fulfillment of the divine purpose in Jesus Christ is appropriated to us individually by the ministry and in the power of the Spirit. It need hardly be pointed out that baptism has always been closely associated with the Spirit. The specific mark of Christ's baptism in distinction from John's is that it is baptism not only with water but also with the Holy Spirit and with fire.[1] When Christ was baptized by John the voice spoke from heaven and the Spirit descended upon him.[2] The regeneration signified by the baptism of water is expressly stated to be the work of the Holy Spirit.[3] When the Holy Spirit was poured out on Cornelius and his company Peter recognized at once that they could not be forbidden water baptism.[4] The more detailed statements in Romans 6 and

[1]Matthew 3:11
[2]Matthew 3:16
[3]John 1:13; 3:5–6
[4]Acts 10:45–48

especially in Romans 8 clearly show that the whole baptismal work of inward mortification and renewal, far from being a purely human possibility, is from first to last the operation of the Holy Spirit.

It should be noted, of course, that the connecting link between baptism and the Holy Spirit is Jesus Christ. The Holy Spirit does not work independently of the Son or the Father any more than the Son works independently of the Father or the Spirit. The Spirit is the Spirit of Christ,[5] is sent by Christ,[6] and bears witness to Christ.[7] Conversely it was by the Spirit that Christ was conceived in his earthly life.[8] The first association of the Spirit with water baptism was when he descended on Christ at his baptism by John.[9] It was in the power of the Spirit that Christ carried through the covenant purpose of God in his life, word, and work and then supremely in his crucifixion and resurrection. "Through the eternal Spirit [he] offered himself without spot to God,"[10] and he was raised again in the power of the same Spirit.[11] In its declaration of the work of the Holy Spirit, baptism speaks to us primarily and principally of that work in its relation to Jesus Christ and his vicarious accomplishment of reconciliation.

Yet the ministry of the Holy Spirit does not end there, for the risen and ascended Christ received from the Father the promise of the Spirit and distributed the gifts and graces of the Spirit to his church.[12] The purpose of this

[5]Romans 8:9
[6]John 16:7
[7]John 16:14
[8]Luke 1:35
[9]Matthew 3:16
[10]Hebrews 9:14
[11]Romans 1:4; 1 Peter 3:18
[12]Acts 2:33

66

imparting of the Spirit can be described in many ways, just as spiritual gifts take many different forms for different detailed ends. In the last analysis, however, it all seems to come back to what Paul calls our being made conformable to Christ,[13] to our participation in his death and resurrection, or to what John describes as our union with him.[14] It is in fact the office of the Holy Spirit, by the word of the gospel and spiritual gifts, to bring about the dying and rising again with Christ which, as we have seen, is our personal identification with the death and resurrection of Christ for us.

Now this is what baptism signifies on its secondary but very necessary "subjective" side. We cannot separate it, of course, from the vicarious action of Christ which is the "objective" side. If we do, it has no substance or meaning. Nor must we give it the primary emphasis, for it is only because Christ has first died and risen again for us in the Spirit that in the power of the same Spirit we can be buried with him and walk in newness of life. Nevertheless, as Christ died and rose again for us, by the Spirit we must, can, and do die and rise again with him. This personal dying and rising again with Christ by the Spirit is brought out in baptism by the fact that it is the individual "I" that is set under the water of baptism and brought out again from the drowning and life-giving water to newness of life in Christ. Baptism is not just *any* baptism; it is *my* baptism. It is my own entry by the word and Spirit into Christ's vicarious work. It is my own identification with him, so that I can now say with the apostle: "He loved me and gave himself for me."[15]

[13]Romans 12:2; Philippians 3:10-11
[14]John 17:20-26
[15]Galatians 2:20

67

This identification with Christ in death and resurrection comes to its first concrete and conscious expression in conversion as the movement of repentance and faith—the turning *from* the old life of sin and the turning *to* the new life of righteousness. It is here that we come up against the basic objection to infant baptism once again. It might be conceded that baptism is not primarily a confession of faith or a first step of obedience. It might be agreed that it bears supreme and proper testimony to the gracious election of the Father and the vicarious reconciliation of the Son. Yet is it not still true that it also bears testimony to the inward regeneration of the Spirit involving personal identification in conscious repentance and faith? Does this not mean that, even if God wills the salvation of infants and declares their covenant status, and even if Christ died and rose again representatively to accomplish their salvation and fulfill the covenant to which they belong, there is still no point in administering to them what must also be a sacrament of personal identification when clearly there neither is nor can be as yet any evidence or expression of conversion, of individual repentance and faith?

The objection is a strong one for two reasons. 1. As we have seen at the outset, there can be no doubting the fact that when the gospel is preached to pagans a definite conversion, or, more precisely, a definite profession of conversion constitutes a prerequisite of baptism. It should again be remembered, however, that in evangelistic mission, baptism will not normally be desired where there is no conversion or profession. 2. It cannot be disputed that when baptism is given prior to individual repentance and faith—and this too we have already noted—it can and does very easily give rise to formalism, false security, and an illusory Christianity which may distort and demolish authentic faith and discipleship. This is especially true in highly sacramentalist systems where the finished work is seen in the regeneration of the infant by the sacrament itself instead of in the vicarious death and resurrection of Christ. Even on a non-sacramentalist view, however, the need for personal identification with Christ may often be blunted. For this reason it is good that infant baptism always be accompanied by the baptism of evangelized adults with its heavier stress on the aspect of personal decision and its clearcut call for individual repentance and faith. Indeed, it is a pity that positions hardened as they did in the Reformation period and that the Reformation churches did not find a place for the Baptist witness, as they now have been forced to do by the increased scale of modern apostasy.

Yet that is not the end of the story. For even in the personal application, identification, or participation, we are not dealing primarily with the individual confession or consciousness of faith but with the regenerative activity of the Holy Spirit, so that even in this sphere the word "subjective" should be used only with careful qualification. In this connection the New Testament example of Cornelius is most instructive and should serve as a warning against hasty conclusions. For in the case of Cornelius we read that the Holy Spirit descended in visible power with no mention at all of a preceding process of repentance and faith.[16] The point is not, of course, that repentance and faith are sometimes unnecessary, but that we ourselves do not control or altogether understand the underlying operation by which they come into being and of which they are the fruit and expression. "The wind bloweth where it

[16]Acts 10:44–48

listeth, and thou hearest the sound thereof, but canst not tell whence it cometh, and whither it goeth: so is every one that is born of the Spirit."[17] Even in our self-identification with Christ what is at issue is not just a work done by us but first and supremely a work done to us and in us on which the work done by us is grounded. What baptism signifies, along with the election of the Father and the reconciliation of the Son, is the regeneration of the Spirit.

The bearing of this is fourfold. 1. We are obviously in no position to say that in any given case the confession or consciousness of faith is either coincident or even identical with the regenerative activity of the Holy Spirit. This point need not be labored—we have touched on it already and it is surely clear enough in itself. Yet it is important enough to merit some expansion. Scripture provides a warning, and Christian history illustrates its truth, that there is such a thing as a purely human belief which can be induced by such purely human methods as propaganda, eloquence, logic, personality, social pressure, and even persecution. People can have a vivid enough awareness of this kind of belief and can make a profession of it which is credible not only to others but also to themselves. Like the tare in the parable, such a belief may often be hard to distinguish from the good plant of authentic faith. Yet it is not regeneration by the Holy Spirit nor a fruit or demonstration of it. For all the consciousness and confession, the person who has it does not have the thing signified in baptism, which is the inner working of the Spirit.

2. Along the same lines we must be careful not to think of faith merely in human terms, as though it were just a

[17]John 3:8

rational possibility and activity of the mind, will, and emotions. If we analyze faith psychologically and phenomenologically we shall find that it is this. But even as we do so, the secret of faith has still eluded us. We penetrate this secret when we turn to scripture and find that saving faith in Jesus Christ is the gift and work of God.[18] Neither grace, salvation, nor faith is of ourselves; it is all God's gift.[19] But the gift and work of God by the Holy Spirit are supernatural. They express themselves, of course, in terms of the human mind, will, and emotions. Behind them, however, is the suprahuman and sovereign factor without which there can be neither the actuality nor the possibility of faith. This factor is the Holy Spirit. It is to the sovereign activity of the Holy Spirit in regeneration, not to the human aspect, to the consciousness of faith or to faith as a human reality, that witness is made in baptism at the level of personal identification with Christ.

3. This leads us to the vital point that we have no right to say that our consciousness or confession of faith is the beginning of the genuine inward activity of the Holy Spirit. It may be true that when adults are converted from paganism the initial work of dying and rising again with Christ takes place only when there is a conscious identification with him in repentance and faith. Yet even in such cases, especially where there is some degree of Christianization, the Holy Spirit may have begun his regenerative work at a much earlier stage. In the momentary thrill of conversion, people are often impatient at much of the instruction that they have perhaps received but which they have failed to understand. They are unconscious,

18Cf. Matthew 16:17; I Corinthians 12:3
19Ephesians 2:8

therefore, of earlier pricks of the Spirit. Only as they grow older and wiser in years and faith do they begin to realize that the Holy Spirit was working in them long before they were ever aware of that work or gave evidence of it. During the entire time that they were in some way in touch with the word of God, and possibly within the prayers of Christians, they were also under the regenerative witness, influence, and operation of the Holy Spirit. To borrow an illustration from the incarnation, as is most fitting, conception by the Spirit and growing in the Spirit preceded actual birth of the Spirit.

In the case of those brought up from infancy in the sphere of the gospel this "conception" can very well go back to infant baptism when prayer is made by minister, parents, and congregation that this work should be done and when a commitment is also entered into that every effort should be made by instruction in the word to bring the child to a knowledge of Christ and to faith in him. In this sense regeneration begins even though birth itself, in terms of a coming to personal faith, does not take place until five, ten, twenty, fifty, or seventy years later. Hence it is supremely fitting that in the covenant context baptism should be administered from the very first. Baptism as identification with Christ is the sacrament of the regenerative work of the Holy Spirit, not of my consciousness and confession of faith. It is the sign of faith only as this is itself the work of the primary and sovereign divine operation.

4. The final implication is that, since faith is the suprahuman operation of the Spirit, it can be given even when there is no normal consciousness of it and even when self-consciousness as such has not yet developed. A favorite debating point of the sixteenth-century Anabap-

tists, still heard in many circles today, was that infants ought not to be baptized because they cannot have faith. Faith, it was argued, demands the self-conscious operation of rational, volitional, and emotional capacities, which is totally outside the sphere of infant possibilities. Luther attempted a reply to the objection at its own humanistic level by pointing out that if faith cannot be present without the self-conscious operation of the faculties, then adults cease to have faith every time they fall asleep and lose it altogether if they go into a final coma. Unfortunately this clever reply ran up against the even cleverer retort of Menno Simons that while adults can certainly have faith when they are asleep we do not baptize them in sleep. But there are two more scriptural considerations.

First, the faith which justifies and saves is not a human possibility, the work of flesh and blood, but a divine reality, the sovereign work of the Spirit, who does not find it at all impossible to reveal the things of God to babes.[20] Indeed, as Luther also pointed out, it is no more a miracle for the Holy Spirit to work in the less resistant hearts of infants than it is for him to work in the self-opinionated and sin-hardened hearts of adults. Precisely because of their self-conscious possibilities, adults are dead in trespasses and sins.[21] For despite all their vaunted faculties, they have of themselves no understanding in this area.[22] Only a rationalistic mind, even though it be the rationalistic mind of a believer, can foolishly suppose that adults enjoy some native possibility of faith whereas infants are such impossible subjects that even the Holy Spirit cannot

[20]Luke 10:21
[21]Ephesians 2:1-3
[22]1 Corinthians 2:6-9

begin his work in them if he so chooses, or indeed bring them to a real faith of which they will not have awareness until later years should they attain a self-conscious life. Surely the Holy Spirit laughs at this so-called possibility and impossibility, just as he laughs at all man's pretentious possibilities and all his solemn judgments on such impossibilities as the virgin birth or the resurrection of Christ from the dead. Who are we to tell the Holy Spirit what he can and cannot do? Regeneration and faith are never a human possibility—they are always in all people a miracle of sovereign grace and power, so that if we think in rationalistic terms we shall always be forced to cry out with Mary[23] or Nicodemus:[24] "How can these things be?" The answer is still the same. No explanation of the mode of operation is given, but "with God all things are possible." He does what he chooses to do and therefore these things are.

But are they? Do we know for a fact that the Holy Spirit works in infants? Here is our second consideration. We might, of course, abstractly attribute all kinds of things to God on the grounds that he can do them. Transubstantiation was frequently defended along these lines. It may seem impossible to us but it is no impossibility to God. The real question, then, is not whether God *can* do a thing but whether he *does* it. In the instance of God's work in infants, however, we have an impossibility which he not only can do but according to the biblical records does do. Infants have in fact been the subjects of the sovereign operation of the Holy Spirit.

In the Old Testament, for example, God says this

[23]Luke 1:34
[24]John 3:4, 9

74

concerning Jeremiah: "Before thou camest forth from the womb I sanctified thee, and I ordained thee a prophet unto the nations."[25] The case of John the Baptist is even more explicit: "He shall be filled with the Holy Ghost, even from his mother's womb."[26] Our Lord, whose humanity was at all points like ours, apart from sin, might also be adduced in this connection.[27] Even Paul, who had so vivid a conversion experience, was conscious that he had in effect been separated from his mother's womb[28] so that if he had been born of Christian parents there would have been no real incongruity in his baptism as an infant. In spite of his years of opposition to the gospel he was still a recipient of the Spirit's activity, and even when he was kicking against the pricks[29] was being fashioned not only as a believer but also as a chosen vessel in the mission of the primitive church.[30] What is established by these examples is that the Holy Spirit not only can work but does work in infants who have not yet attained self-consciousness or even birth. Possibly there were special circumstances in these instances. Possibly the work of the Holy Spirit here was a highly specific work. We cannot say for certain, but we can say that it was undoubtedly a work in infants and that all the work of the Spirit is a special and miraculous work, so that in the so-called normal instances of infancy a regenerative ministry is by no means to be excluded. If there is a believing community, the prayer of faith, and commitment to an upbringing under the word of

[25]Jeremiah 1:5
[26]Luke 1:15
[27]Cf. Luke 1:32–35
[28]Galatians 1:15
[29]Acts 26:14
[30]Acts 9:15

God by which the Spirit works, we have indeed no reason not to expect that the regenerative work of the Spirit will begin according to his sovereign disposing. Certainly the sign of this action should not be denied on the ground of an alleged impossibility of the thing signified.

Discussion of these points has taken us rather far afield from the main theme of being made conformable to Christ in his vicarious work. Yet if it has established the nature of regeneration as the initiation of this identification in the power and sovereignty of the Holy Spirit, a useful purpose has been served. It has shown us that in a covenant context it is unnecessary and even foolish to insist on a temporal link between conscious faith on the one hand and the regenerative operation of the Spirit, and therefore the sign of that operation, on the other. We must now revert to the main question and in so doing see that regeneration, as a work of the sovereign Spirit, has a significance extending far beyond itself, for it is the first stage of a renewal in Christ which will be completed only on the last day. The same applies, therefore, to the outworking of regeneration in repentance and faith which are the beginning and not the end of identification with the death and resurrection of Christ. Baptism, as the sign of regeneration and faith, also has this wider significance and scope, reaching beyond the initial movement with which it is so often almost exclusively associated.

7
The Scope
of Baptism

BAPTISM DECLARES the inward regenerative operation of the Holy Spirit which makes us conformable to
Jesus Christ. In its full compass this operation includes
endowment with gifts and graces for the service of God,
for a life in identification with Jesus Christ will naturally
and necessarily be a life of service as was the life of Jesus.
Basically, however, it consists in the movement of death
and rising again as participation in the death and rising
again of Christ. Applied to us, death and rising again mean
remission of sins and regeneration, with both of which
baptism is expressly connected in the New Testament.
The remission of sins is the cancelling of the old life of
sin, and regeneration is the beginning of the new and
eternal life of righteousness. In the power of the Holy
Spirit, therefore, we are inserted or initiated into Christ's
crucifixion and resurrection, so that we personally, in and
with the company of all believers, die to sin and rise again
to righteousness in enjoyment of the benefits of Christ's
work of vicarious reconciliation.

Now when we consult Holy Scripture we find that this work of initiation or insertion is not presented merely as the work of a moment. It may certainly be understood as a single act, but one with three successive stages. Dying and rising again with Christ cannot be identified wholly or exclusively with any one of these stages. In particular, it cannot be identified wholly and exclusively with an isolated experience of conversion, important though this undoubtedly is in creating all things new. Dying and rising again with Christ is a whole process of renewal or new creation and at every point this process is the work of the Holy Spirit as he identifies us with Jesus Christ. A common pattern runs through the whole process which shows that it is a unified work. This is the pattern of dying and renewal which is so clearly declared in baptism. In its witness to the reconciling work of God the Son and the regenerating work of God the Holy Spirit, baptism is the sign and seal of the total fulfillment of the election of God the Father and is also a summons to the baptized to enter into the totality of the divine activity. Baptism tells us what has been done, what is being done, and what will be done for us, to us, and in us. God has elected us and reconciled us to himself and is now refashioning us in the image of Christ. Baptism also tells us in the power of the Spirit what we are to do in response. "Be ye reconciled to God."[1] "Be imitators of me, as I am of Christ."[2]

Now obviously the actual moment of new birth, which finds its counterpart in conversion or the coming to faith, forms the first stage of identification with Jesus Christ. At this first stage the old and sinful self is replaced by the

---

[1] 2 Corinthians 5:20
[2] 1 Corinthians 11:1 (RSV)

new and righteous self which is born of the Spirit. In terms of conversion, this means a turning away from self in repentance and a turning to Jesus Christ in faith. This stage of regeneration or conversion has all the significance of a beginning and in this case has a special significance as God's work, for in a sense it already includes the whole. Even when viewed from the standpoint of the believer it is the entry into a finished work of reconciliation and regeneration. The end, therefore, is given to us with the beginning. Once we are in Jesus Christ by repentance and faith we can say with confidence, though not, of course, with self-boasting, that we are justified,[3] that we are risen,[4] that we are a new creation,[5] and that we have eternal life.[6] For, as we read in Hebrews 11:1: "Faith is the substance of things hoped for, the evidence of things not seen."

Because conversion, or the moment of new birth, has this very special significance, a very strong connection exists between it and baptism. We must be careful, however, not to understand or state this connection in the wrong way. Baptism, as we have noted, is not primarily the witness, sign, or seal of my own consciousness and confession of repentance and faith. It is first and foremost the witness, sign, and seal of what the Father elected for me, of what the Son did in my place, and of what the Spirit is doing in and to me. Conversion has to be seen, then, in its proper context. Its significance lies in the fact that it is a fulfillment of the election of the Father, an identification with the reconciling death and resurrection

[3]Romans 5:1
[4]Colossians 3:3
[5]2 Corinthians 5:17
[6]John 3:36

of the Son, and a first outworking of the regenerative operation of the Holy Spirit which carries with it the assurance of the continuation and completion of this work and a summons to its ongoing expression in a lifelong identification with Christ.

How does this work out in relation to the baptized? Adults converted from paganism or unbelief are baptized as they profess their faith in the first step of identification—the moment of the new birth. Previously they cannot be baptized; they are outside the sphere of the word and the Spirit. They have no desire for baptism, and it has no meaning for them. But now that they have heard and received the gospel promises, now that the Holy Spirit has done in them the work which leads to repentance and faith, and now that a beginning has been made of participation in Christ, baptism takes on meaning as a testimony, seal, and confirmation. It bears witness to what they do, but it also shows them that their actions have deeper meaning than just a human decision or a change of religious belief and practice. In repentance and faith there is fulfilled the regeneration in us which will bring to personal completion the electing and reconciling work of God for us.

The situation differs with the children of confessing Christians. From the very beginning they are in the sphere of the word and Spirit, and the prayer of parents and congregation is made for them. They are not necessarily converted, and baptism itself will not convert them, but the gospel promises are before them and every reason exists to believe that the Holy Spirit has begun his work within them. They thus receive baptism as a sign and seal of the divine election, reconciliation, and regeneration. As they grow older, they may come quickly to individual repentance and faith. On the other hand they may move away for a period, or perhaps forever. But baptism is always there, bearing its witness to the will of the Father, the work of the Son, and the ministry of the Spirit. The church's proclamation tells them what they are to do. They are to die and rise again with Christ in personal repentance and faith, and are to begin the outworking of their renewal in conversion. In this personal application conversion is now the first objective. Baptism has now an evangelistic office as an adjunct of the word. It tells those who are baptized as children that it will find actualization in them only as the first stage of the Spirit's work is reached and they come to repentance and faith. When they do so it again serves as a necessary reminder and reassurance that this is not just a human decision but a deep work of God. Until they do, however, it is a continual pointer to the act that they must perform as those within the sphere of the Holy Spirit. As an act which has been performed on them, baptism, like the gospel message which they have been taught, is something that they may ignore and forget in resistance to the Spirit's ministry and the church's prayer and plea. But if they do ignore and forget it, it will witness against them on the day of judgment. God made his elective covenant with them, Christ accomplished his vicarious work of reconciliation for them, and the Holy Spirit willed to perform his regenerative ministry in them, but like Esau they despised their birthright, exchanging it for a mess of pottage.

Conversion, then, is the first step. It has special importance as such. In isolation, however, it is in no sense the end or the totality of the Spirit's work of conforming us to the death and resurrection of Christ. In no sense does it exhaust the meaning of baptism from the standpoint of the regenerative ministry of the Spirit. The new birth, like natural birth, has its own significance, but not apart from the life into which one is born. Regeneration in the sense of actual entry into the new life in Christ forms part of the entire process of renewal which continues throughout the whole period of the Christian's life on earth. Conversion as the first turning is a necessary beginning yet it carries with it the ongoing process of turning from sin and turning to Christ, of putting off the old man and putting on the new,[7] which is the special meaning of the Christian life. Here again we have to identify with Christ in his death and resurrection. This process is a continual dying to sin and rising again to righteousness on the basis of Christ's vicarious act of reconciliation and in the power of the regenerative and re-creative ministry of the Holy Spirit.

The Epistles in particular are full of this theme. Thus we are told that "if ye through the Spirit do mortify the deeds of the body, ye shall live."[8] We are not to be "conformed to this world" but "transformed by the renewing of our mind."[9] Again, we are to "put off concerning the former conversation the old man," to be "renewed in the spirit of our mind," and to "put on the new man, which after God is created in righteousness and true holiness."[10] The goal of the Christian life is to know Christ, "and the power of his resurrection, and the fellowship of his sufferings, being made conformable unto his death."[11] We must work out the putting off of the old man and the putting on of the new in the mortification of "our members which are

[7]Ephesians 4:22–24
[8]Romans 8:13
[9]Romans 12:2
[10]Ephesians 4:22–24
[11]Philippians 3:10

upon the earth."[12] This will take place in sufferings as well as in self-discipline, and we can rejoice that "though our outward man perish, yet the inward man is renewed day by day."[13] Naturally this message can be understood in its full range and depth only in the light of the death and resurrection of Christ on our behalf. Nevertheless, it is securely rooted in Christ's own teaching: "If any man will come after me, let him deny himself,"[14] or again: "Whosoever he be of you that forsaketh not all that he hath, he cannot be my disciple,"[15] or even perhaps: "If thy hand offend thee, cut it off."[16]

What is the relation of all this to baptism? There is, of course, an implicit connection. Baptism bears witness to the death and resurrection of Christ into which we are to enter not only in repentance and faith but also in daily mortification and renewal. This implicit connection is made explicit, however, in the great baptismal passage in Romans 6, where Paul introduces the thought of baptismal death and resurrection as a summons to its outworking in Christian conduct. The apostle's argument seems to be as follows. Baptism into Jesus Christ is baptism into his death and burial for us. In him we are already dead and buried. Accepting this fact in penitence and faith, we know that our old self is crucified with Christ so that the body of sin might be destroyed. With this knowledge we are thus challenged to reckon ourselves to be dead indeed to sin and alive to God, not yielding our members as instruments of unrighteousness to sin, but yielding our-

[12]Colossians 3:5
[13]2 Corinthians 4:16
[14]Matthew 16:24
[15]Luke 14:33
[16]Mark 9:43

selves to God as those who are alive from the dead, and our members as instruments of righteousness to God. In other words, baptism as the attestation of our death and resurrection in and with Christ carries a reference to the whole life of the Christian. If it is an evangelistic summons to children born in the covenant sphere of the word and Spirit, to them and to converted adults as well it has ethical significance as a significatory spur to ongoing mortification and renewal.

Again, however, baptism must not be construed as the sign of a purely human decision and work. It was here, perhaps, that the Anabaptists lost their way. No one bore brighter or more consistent witness to the fact that baptism is an initiation into discipleship, into a way of life that carries with it suffering and renewal. Yet they deduced from this that no one ought to be baptized without a steadfast determination and commitment to take up this course of life and to pursue it to the end. Their emphasis tended to fall on the human aspect. Mortification and renewal, however, are more than a venture in human ethics. They are the continuation of the regenerating or re-creative ministry of the Holy Spirit. Christians themselves, of course, are engaged in this work. We cannot escape or minimize the personal reference. The Holy Spirit will not and does not deal with us as automatons here any more than when he brings us to individual repentance and faith. Nevertheless, this work of mortification and renewal is not a possibility or achievement of our own. We are engaged in it only because Jesus Christ has already done it for us and the Holy Spirit is doing it in us. As Paul puts it, it is because we are already dead in Christ that we are to mortify our members. In Galatians,[17] and especially in

[17]Galatians 5:16–18

Romans 8 and Philippians, he makes it plain that this working out of salvation in ethical reconstruction is through the Holy Spirit: "If ye through the Spirit do mortify the deeds of the body, ye shall live";[18] "It is God which worketh in you both to will and to do of his good pleasure."[19]

For our part we learn from the sacrament of baptism what this work of the Spirit is and what identification with Christ means for us in terms of daily life and service. Whether we are baptized as infants or adults makes little difference at this stage. The meaning and message of baptism are the same. None of us can claim that witness is given in baptism to the actual achievement of the ongoing work of baptism in personal life. At most the subjective side can consist only in a commitment to its future fulfillment. In this pledge alone, not in an actual performance, can a right to baptism be sought. For all of us baptism is in this respect an assurance that our sanctification is a fact accomplished vicariously in Jesus Christ and that its outworking in our lives is to become a present reality in the renewing operation of the Holy Spirit. For all of us, too, baptism is here a summons to be what we are, to enter more and more into the fullness of identification with Christ in his death and resurrection, which in terms of its actualization in daily life and conduct is an ongoing process and thus has always a future as well as a past and present reference.

Nor is this the closing stage. Birth leads on through growth to fullness or maturity. Beyond conversion and ongoing sanctification lies the completion of the Christian life when we enter into the full actuality of the new life in

[18]Romans 8:13
[19]Philippians 2:13

Christ which is even now our true reality and calling. Again, and this time totally and finally, we are in the sphere of identification with Christ in his death and resurrection. On the basis of Christ's vicarious work of reconciliation and in the strength of the Spirit's sovereign ministry of regeneration, we will ultimately be dead in the body and resurrected in a new and spiritual body to the fullness of the new creation and eternal life in Christ.

The New Testament is full of references to this eschatological dimension. In Romans 8, for example, Paul moves from a consideration of the present work of the Spirit to the hoped for and assured redemption: "Ourselves also, which have the firstfruits of the Spirit, even we ourselves groan within ourselves, waiting for the adoption, to wit, the redemption of our body."[20] Or again in 1 Corinthians 15 he speaks at large of the final destiny of Christ's people when this corruptible must put on incorruption and this mortal immortality.[21] Ephesians also points ahead to the redemption of the purchased possession.[22] Hebrews describes it as one of the functions of faith to look forward to a better resurrection.[23] Peter, too, reminds his readers of "an inheritance incorruptible, and that fadeth not away, reserved in heaven for you, who are kept by the power of God through faith unto salvation ready to be revealed in the last time."[24] This witness undoubtedly goes back to the teaching of Christ himself when he spoke so clearly of our redemption at his coming again[25] and also of the resurrection of the dead, which is

[20]Romans 8:23
[21]1 Corinthians 15:53–54
[22]Ephesians 1:13–14
[23]Hebrews 11:35
[24]1 Peter 1:4–5
[25]Luke 21:28

not at all excluded or replaced by the present possession of eternal life.[26]

The implied relation to baptism hardly needs to be indicated, for again the theme is that of death and resurrection, the basis is the vicarious dying and rising again of Christ, and the power is that of the life-giving Spirit who does for us here what we patently cannot do for ourselves, both enabling us to die in the Lord and also raising us up again to eternal life in the spiritual body. Here again, however, there are one or two more explicit references. One of them is the obscure saying in 1 Corinthians 15:29. Probably the exact meaning of this statement will always be something of a mystery. Nevertheless, although commentators differ widely in their detailed suggestions, there can be little disagreement on one point. Baptism arises in this passage because of a definite connection which it bears in some way to physical dissolution and resurrection. In baptism we see both death and rising again. The saying in Ephesians 1:13 is ambivalent as well, for not every exegete would accept a reference to baptism. It seems difficult, however, to perceive how sealing with the Holy Spirit can be anything else, or, if it is, what that something else is. If the reference is to baptism, or to the work of the Holy Spirit which is the thing signified in baptism, then the general thought is similar to that of Romans 8. God will complete the work which he has begun in us. Hence the outward sign and seal of that work declares not only the first instalment but also the final redemption of which it is the pledge.

The linking of baptism with the resurrection is significant. It means that baptism, like the Lord's Supper, is given as a sign for the period between the accomplishment

[26]John 6:39–40

of our salvation in Christ's representative death and resurrection and his coming again when we who have died in the physical body shall be raised again in the new spiritual body. Baptism has a backward look to the vicarious death and resurrection of Christ and a forward look to his triumphant coming again with his transformed and risen people. Between these, it carries a present reference to our identification with Christ in faith and sanctification which is the particular outworking in the intervening days of grace.

The fact that baptism has this forward-looking aspect means, of course, that whether we be baptized as infants or as adults, the personal application cannot be fulfilled nor the work of the Spirit completed prior to the administration of the sacrament. This completion or fulfillment must wait until the faith of conversion gives way to the sight of resurrection. Baptism is a sign whose significance can never be exhausted in this life. It speaks to us of the new birth as our initial entry into Christ and his work on our behalf. It speaks to us of lifelong renewal as our ongoing identification with Christ and his substitutionary dying and rising again. It also speaks to us of the resurrection as our definitive participation in Christ and the death and resurrection that he underwent vicariously for us.

This baptismal reference to the resurrection as our final entry into Christ and the new life in him helps us to see and grasp more clearly two important truths which have constantly presented themselves to us in the course of this study. 1. The first is that baptism must not be self-centeredly treated as primarily the witness to some decision or activity of our own. Apart from hastening our dissolution—if that is any help!—there is indeed no contribution that we can make, whether by commitment or by action, to our being raised again from the dead. Here is a sovereign and miraculous act of the Creator Spirit for which we can only wait, for which we can only pray, and in which we can only trust. In relation to conversion and sanctification the temptation can easily arise to allow what we do to play the central role, as though regeneration and ongoing renewal were a human possibility for which no more than a little cooperation of God with our own will and action were required. In relation to the resurrection from the dead, however, this temptation can find no foothold except among those who foolishly try to transform the kingdom of Christ into an ultimate earthly utopia, and even then the past and present generations can have no hope of participation except by the contribution they might make to it. The granting of resurrection life is solely and exclusively a divine possibility and prerogative. To be sure, the resurrection will be mine, worked out in terms of my personal self. In this it resembles conversion and sanctification. But again, it is my resurrection only on the basis of the resurrection of Christ for me, not on the basis of any inherent quality in me nor of any merit or achievement, not even in conversion or sanctification. It is also my resurrection only in the power of the regenerative and life-giving Spirit, not in the power of any inherent potential nor of any activity or contribution of my own, not even in the life of faith and love and hope. The activity which baptism signifies and seals is first, last, solely, and supremely the activity of the electing Father, the reconciling Son, and the regenerating Spirit.

2. The second truth is that not one of us can say: I have a right to baptism because the work of which it speaks has already been fulfilled in me and I am thus declaring that here and now I am identified in this way with Jesus Christ. Whether we be baptized in infancy or

on profession of faith, there is in fact no time when we can say that baptism refers simply to some past or present experience in our own life and that it has meaning and value solely or primarily as a witness to that experience. As a sign of the regenerating, renewing, and resurrecting work of the Holy Spirit it always has a wider as well as a narrower time reference. It begins with Christ's first coming before our present life and it ends with his coming again after our present life. Thus we begin with Christ's death and resurrection for us and we end with our own death and resurrection with him at the last day. Our attainment of this end is the creative work of the Holy Spirit which is declared to us in baptism and which has its initial outworking in conversion and the ongoing movement of renewal. Only when the end has been attained can we say that by the work of the Spirit we have fully entered into the baptism of Christ. But then the thing signified will be present in its totality and the sign and its testimony will no longer be needed.

8
The Salvation
of Infants

W E HAVE NOW CONSIDERED some basic reasons for
a valid evangelical continuation of infant baptism. Before
we leave the topic, however, one question demands more
specific treatment, a question which has been implicit in
all our previous deliberations. This is the question of infant salvation. Can we believe that infants, or at any rate
some infants, share the blessings of salvation even though
they die before having the chance to come to a conscious
decision of repentance and faith? Have we any scriptural
guidance on this matter or is it simply an area for pious
speculation? In countries with a low incidence of infant
mortality the subject is not so urgent as it once was. Indeed, it may appear to be of greater theoretical than practical interest. Over the whole range of Christian geography
and history, however, it is a very relevant and pressing
matter, for a high proportion of the world's population has
in fact died in infancy or early childhood. The question
may also help us to bring our baptismal theology into a
final and sharper focus, for infant baptism and infant salva-

tion are clearly interrelated. If there can be no salvation of infants in default of a conscious decision and confession, the administration of infant baptism will obviously make very little sense for anyone. If, on the other hand, infants can enjoy the work of God as the thing signified by the baptismal sign, it is difficult to see what good or proper reason there is for denying them the sign.

The scriptural evidence need not detain us long, for it consists mainly of passages to which reference has already been made. In the New Testament, as we recall, the Lord Jesus Christ makes some very definite and almost startling declarations about children. Some of them have no doubt a partly parabolic character: "Except ye be converted, and become as little children, ye shall not enter into the kingdom of heaven";[1] "I thank thee, O Father, Lord of heaven and earth, that thou hast hid these things from the wise and prudent, and hast revealed them unto babes."[2] Even so, it is not insignificant that our Lord selected a child in illustration of these matters concerning the renewing and enlightening work of the Holy Spirit. In other instances there is undoubtedly a more precise and direct reference to infants as such: "Suffer the little children to come unto me, and forbid them not: for of such is the kingdom of God";[3] "Whoso shall receive one such little child in my name receiveth me. But whoso shall offend one of these little ones which believe in me, it were better for him that a millstone were hanged about his neck, and that he were drowned in the depth of the sea."[4] Whatever may be the ultimate thrust or interpretation of these say-

[1]Matthew 18:3
[2]Luke 10:21
[3]Mark 10:14
[4]Matthew 18:5–6

92

ings, we may surely say with confidence that Christ himself did not envisage an exclusion of little children from salvation or an impossibility of childlike faith in him. This conclusion is supported by the Pauline reference to the "holiness" of children and by the biblical examples of infants who from the very first were sanctified or even filled by the Holy Spirit.

The Old Testament evidence all points in the same direction. This is especially true of its teaching that children belong to the covenant people, are redeemed with it, circumcised, and given early instruction in its beliefs and practices. It is also significant that some of the most tremendous prophecies of the Old Testament point ahead to the coming of the Messiah in the form of a child: "For unto us a child is born, unto us a son is given."[5] Christ in his humanity was to become an infant, the babe of Bethlehem, with no more self-awareness than other infants, yet not on that account deprived of his fellowship with the Father and the Holy Spirit. The second-century writer Irenaeus was not altogether fanciful when he suggested that Christ identified himself with all the stages of human life from infancy to maturity in order that there might be salvation and identification with Christ at every stage. Indeed, is it not significant that we read of the redeemed creation: "A little child shall lead them"?[6]

The point need not be pressed, for few indeed have thought that infants cannot be and are not saved at all. There has been a widespread belief that since baptism is the appointed and indispensable means of salvation, unbaptized infants who die in infancy go to perdition. In this

[5] Isaiah 9:6; cf. 7:14
[6] Isaiah 11:6

school of thought, however, baptized infants are obviously thought to be saved and even the unbaptized are often seen as undergoing a mitigated punishment or even enjoying a lesser salvation.

If, however, it has been almost universally conceded by Christians that infants can be and are saved, we must engage in a deeper probe. On what grounds and by what means are they saved? This is obviously a critical question, not merely for our understanding of infant baptism, but for our whole conception of the gospel, especially in its relation to the elective decision of the Father, the reconciling work of the Son, and the regenerative ministry of the Spirit.

A first answer, which is not to be summarily dismissed, is the sacramentalist one. This has provoked vigorous reactions because of its handling of the instrumentality of baptism, for it postulates both an automatic efficacy and an absolute necessity of the sacrament in the case of infants. If, however, these infringements on the divine freedom are set aside, the sacramentalist understanding shows a firm grasp of certain important truths. It cannot exempt infants from the collective responsibility of the human race described as original sin. It sees the need for a true work of regeneration in infants as well as adults. It cannot allow salvation for anyone apart from the saving operation of the Triune God. Infants, too, depend on the divine election, reconciliation, and regeneration.

In contrast, the tempting possibility has been held open that infants are saved simply because they are never lost. Obviously they have not, as infants, committed any acts of personal sin. They are thus, it is argued, in the same state of inherent innocence and uprightness as our first parents before the fall. No accusation can be made, or at least sustained, against them. They do not have to be specially elected. They need no divine forgiveness. Participation in Christ's vicarious work of reconciliation is not demanded and regeneration is unnecessary. If they live they will with all probability, and even with certainty, fall into sin and thus incur the need for salvation. They have a propensity to sin and they live in an influential environment of sin. In themselves, however, they are as yet completely innocent. They are said to belong to Christ's kingdom in virtue of this innocence.

According to this understanding there can be no point in giving baptism to infants. This is still true even on a sacramentalist view of baptismal instrumentality, for infants do not need this instrument. They are not excluded from eternal blessedness to begin with. They have no conceivable need of, or title to, the instituted sign of the Father's election, the Son's reconciliation, and the Spirit's regeneration. They neither require nor know the grace, forgiveness, and renewal to which it is the particular office of the ordinance or sacrament of baptism to bear witness. In this regard it is significant that when the fifth-century Pelagians advanced a doctrine of infant innocence they had to find special reasons for continuing to baptize infants. They were opposed, of course, by the crushing if gruesome insistence of Augustine that infants are under damnation until they receive the sacrament of remission and regeneration. It is also significant that many of the sixteenth-century Anabaptists not only had a rationalistic view of the decision of faith but also showed a marked tendency to follow Pelagian ideas of infant uprightness and the freedom of men, even as sinners, to do either good or evil. If infants cannot have unconscious faith, they also cannot have unconscious sin. They are thus saved because they are not yet lost. They have still to forfeit their original innocence. It is thus inappropriate as well as unnecessary to administer to them the sign of salvation, forgiveness, and renewal, or of repentance, faith, and commitment.

Holy Scripture, however, seems to offer little support for this teaching, as even a cursory reading must surely suggest. It insists very strongly and firmly that all people without exception are fallen and guilty sinners. "There is none righteous, no, not one."[7] At the individual level some are far worse sinners than others. Indeed, personal sin can hardly be ascribed to infants. Yet scripture does not view the human race merely as a collection of individuals. If they are not called in isolation, they also do not sin in isolation. The race is bound together in a solidarity of sin from which even infants are not exempt. "Behold, I was shapen in iniquity; and in sin did my mother conceive me."[8] "By one man sin entered into the world, and death by sin; and so death passed upon all men, for that all have sinned."[9] The propensity to sin which all too quickly manifests itself in infants is due to the fact that within the nexus of the race they are already sinners by nature. They do not become sinners by sinning; they sin because they are sinners.

Opinions vary widely as to the detailed outworking of this truth. Some ascribe more importance to heredity and some to environment. Others see a distinction between inherent and imputed sin. Scripture itself maintains a comparative reticence in this regard which we do well to

[7]Romans 3:10; cf. Psalm 14:3
[8]Psalm 51:5
[9]Romans 5:12

imitate, recognizing that in details of this kind we are in the sphere of theorizing or pious opinion. Nevertheless, the Bible leaves us in no shadow of a doubt that adamic man is fallen man. He is not just the man who commits sins. He is the man who commits sins because he is a sinner. As a sinner against God he is guilty before him. Without analyzing it more closely, Paul sums it up in a striking statement: "We are all by nature the children of wrath."[10]

As Holy Scripture finds no exceptions to the rule that all are sinners, so it offers no exceptions to the rule that salvation is by Christ alone and therefore by faith in him. Over against the representative figure of Adam, Paul sets the representative figure of Christ.[11] Christ is the one righteous one who himself bore the sin of the world[12] and who is the head of the new creation.[13] If there is to be salvation at all, it can be only on the ground of his righteousness and atonement. There is no such thing as a righteousness of infants, or of any others, side by side with the righteousness of Christ. Salvation is exclusively by way of the divine forgiveness through Christ's reconciling work. "There is none other name under heaven given among men, whereby we must be saved."[14] This also means, however, that salvation is exclusively by faith in Christ, by the faith which is the work of the Holy Spirit identifying us with Christ. Because we say "by Christ alone" we must also say "by faith alone." "Without faith it is impossible to please God."[15] Infants, like all others, are either saved by

[10]Ephesians 2:3
[11]Romans 5:15–21
[12]John 1:29
[13]1 Corinthians 15:20–23
[14]Acts 4:12
[15]Hebrews 11:6

Christ alone, and therefore by faith in him, or it is hard to see how, in view of the inclusiveness of sin and the exclusiveness of the way of salvation, they can really be saved at all. If, however, infants are saved by Christ and by faith in him, it is also hard to find any intrinsic reason why they should be refused the sacrament of salvation and faith if they are born in the covenant sphere of the word and Spirit.

The question arises, of course, whether we can really say that infants, or at least some infants, are indeed saved by Christ and by faith in him. The first part of the statement does not create too much difficulty when we remember the vicarious nature of Christ's reconciling death and resurrection. Jesus took the place of all. He identified himself with every form and stage and state of humanity. When he died on the cross he took all sin upon himself. "The Lord hath laid on him the iniquity of us all."[16] "He hath made him to be sin for us, who knew no sin."[17] He made an end of the old man of sin and brought in the new man of righteousness. In this representative or substitutionary work of Christ infants and their sinfulness are clearly included. They, too, are sinners in Adam, and are born the old man. But Jesus Christ has taken their place. In his activity for them, they have thus, in him, died as old men, sinners, and been raised up as new men, righteous. They need not be condemned because of their sinfulness in Adam, for there is forgiveness for that sinfulness in the reconciling work of the sinners' substitute. If they cannot be included in salvation because of a pretended innocence, they need not be shut out because of their descent

[16]Isaiah 53:6
[17]2 Corinthians 5:21

98

from Adam, for their life as the children of Adam ended at the cross and in Christ they have a new life as the children of God. As their baptism signifies, this work of the Son has been done for them in fulfillment of the election of the Father.

This much is easy enough to follow. The difficulty arises, not with the first part of the statement, "by Christ," but with the second, "and therefore by faith in him." While we can appreciate that Christ's reconciling work has been done for infants as for all others, can we say with any assurance that they enter into it and share its benefits so that they are saved by faith? Even those who have held this view have often found it necessary to advance some qualifying explanation. Some, for example, speak of a seed of faith rather than faith itself. Others refer to a faith suitable to infant capacities. Still others point to elements of trust which may be shown by infants in the sphere of human relations. All this may be helpful, but surely the true explanation of infant faith and its possibility lies, as we have seen earlier, in the regenerative activity of the Holy Spirit. The faith by which Christ's righteousness becomes ours is not primarily or independently a human decision. It is the gift and work of the Holy Spirit.

Certainly this gift and work of the Holy Spirit is a miracle in infants. But it is equally a miracle in adults. Faith in Christ cannot be regarded as a human possibility. Hence infant faith in Christ cannot be regarded as a divine impossibility. As we have to say that the Holy Spirit alone can and does give faith to adults, so we dare not say that the Holy Spirit has no ability to give faith to infants. Even if to the best of our knowledge infants do not and cannot decide to believe, this is in keeping with their need, for similarly they do not and cannot decide to sin. Nevertheless, in whatever infant awareness they have, as they are sinners in Adam, so by the ministry of the Holy Spirit they can be believers in the children's Savior, who himself was not without fellowship with the Father during the days of his own infancy. The baptism of infants does not signify an infant decision. It signifies the regenerative ministry of the Holy Spirit by which infant faith is possible, and with it an entry into the vicarious reconciliation of the Son according to the election of the Father.

There remain only two further problems. 1. The first is whether this infant salvation applies to all infants and not just to those who die in infancy. If it does, many of those who grow to years of discretion seem to lose their salvation and then have to come to it again by personal repentance and faith. If it does not, are we not in a strange world of uncertainty where infants, and therefore their baptism, are concerned? For who, then, are saved and who are not?

One has to say, however, that in the light of the divine freedom and providence this whole question is superfluous. It is also futile, for it leads us into areas where our ignorance is more conspicuous than our insight and God in his self-revelation has not been pleased to illumine us. All that we need affirm is the twofold fact that infants who die in infancy are saved, although not without infant faith in Christ, while those who grow to self-conscious life need to make a personal decision of penitence and faith, although in many cases this may proceed from a work of the Spirit which dates back much earlier—even back to infancy.

For the rest, we are left in the field of human speculation, which may be interesting but can never be definitive. There are some who claim that original sin is forgiven to all people, which seems most reasonable in the light of the vicarious nature of the work of Christ. Others believe that all infants are saved until they consciously sin or consciously reject Christ, although this raises difficulties in relation to assurance of salvation. Others, as we have seen, focus on a distinction between infant faith and adult faith, which will not necessarily be in continuity, although it is hoped that the one will lead to the other. Suggestions of this kind are obviously not to be pressed. The one thing we know for certain, in relation to both infants and adults, is that "the Lord knoweth them that are his."[18]

It might be noted, incidentally, that this whole problem is not one of infant baptism alone but of all baptism. If we believe, as we surely must, that infants, or at least some infants, are saved, then the fact that we do not know this final secret is no reason for withholding the sacrament in proper cases. For, after all, we do not know much about the salvation of adults who are baptized when they make a profession of faith. They, too, can pursue a checkered course and if the ordinance has to be tied in with what is thought to be real salvation, frequent baptisms may be the result. The fact is that neither in infants nor in adults can our administration of the sacrament be made to hang on the knowledge of the secrets of the heart which God alone can discern.

2. The second problem is whether, on this whole view of infant salvation, baptism ought to be extended to all infants instead of limited to the children of professing Christians. Again the question is for the most part superfluous, for in point of fact pagan parents do not want baptism for their children and the vast majority would very strongly forbid and prevent it. Furthermore, the biblical

[18] 2 Timothy 2:19

material which we surveyed earlier, and which so solidly supports the covenant status of the children of covenant members, provides no authorization at all even to attempt the administration of the covenant signs where God has not yet set his name and where children will not grow up within the promises and ministry of the covenant. This does not, of course, preclude the possibility of the infants of non-Christians being saved, as many evangelical theologians believe and hope they will. What it means is that if these infants do not by descent come visibly within the covenant context they should not be given the sign of the covenant—unless, of course, they are adopted by Christians or come under Christian care. If they die in infancy, they may indeed be saved through Christ's reconciling work and the Spirit's regenerating ministry. Even if they grow older, they may come under the proclamation of the gospel and be brought to repentance and faith. Outside the visible covenant, however, they cannot meaningfully be baptized into the Triune name even if the opportunity for baptism arises, which for all practical purposes it does not.

Many professing Christians, unfortunately, are Christians only in a very loose and nominal sense. This gives rise to the related issue of what is often called indiscriminate baptism. In reality, however, this is more a problem of church discipline than it is of baptism. The scandal—and it is this—can arise only in a badly disciplined church which clearly does not take itself seriously as the church and which in many cases will amount to little more than a thinly christianized society. The remedy, then, should deal with the basic disease and not just the symptom. The place to begin is not with an unwarranted discrimination against infants, who are not responsible, but with an insistence on the proper fulfillment by parents and sponsors of the obligations of their own confession as well as those which they undertake for their children.

If professing Christians live notoriously irreligious, unbelieving, and immoral lives, they should be faced with their sins and errors and given the prescribed opportunities to repent and to give themselves to authentic faith and discipleship. If they openly refuse to do so, they should be properly excommunicated. Where both parents bring on themselves this exclusion from the visible covenant, the rights of their children to the covenant sign will then lapse and baptism will be withheld until the parents repent or the children come to conversion. This proper excommunication should be recognized as well as practiced by all churches.

Sporadic discrimination against infants, however, can never solve a problem which begins elsewhere and which can be met only by effective action by the churches at the appropriate level. If such action is not taken, and indiscipline continues to rule, in the long run the problem may very well solve itself, for nominal Christianity will gradually shade off into practicing unbelief and infants will no longer be presented for baptism. Be that as it may, if the problem arises in the context of baptism, it is not in this context that it should be primarily tackled. As Calvin observed, the title to baptism usually rests on many generations of covenant descent[19] and cannot easily be overthrown by the lapse of a single generation. In baptism, if anywhere, there is good reason for mercy rather than se-

[19]Deuteronomy 7:9

verity, for an emphasis on the covenant faithfulness of God rather than the covenant failure of men. To be sure, there ought to be discipline in the church. But discrimination in the administration of baptism, while it will be the salutary result, should hardly be viewed as the proper starting point.

Conclusion

I T WAS RECOGNIZED at the outset of this study that in the absence of a direct New Testament precept or precedent no definitive ruling can be given in the matter of baptizing or not baptizing infants. Hence the conclusion of the investigation can be only a qualified and not a decisive or exclusive one. It may be stated under the three heads of negative aspects, positive aspects, and practical implications.

On the negative side no evidence has been uncovered to close the gap which gives rise to the problem. This was not unexpected, for if an explicit mandate were present it would have been known to the church across the centuries. In this regard, then, we are at the point where we started. No command to baptize infants has been found nor any direct exclusion from baptism of the children of professing Christians. Similarly no precise instance of infant baptism has been adduced nor has any instance of the later baptism of children born to Christian parents. What does not exist cannot be presented.

Also on the negative side no reason has been found for discontinuing adult baptism. In this regard those who practice infant baptism do not see themselves confronted by an either/or situation. The church cannot be just a self-perpetuating body. It always must be reaching out both to those who have never been evangelized at all and also to those who have not received the gospel even in a partly christianized society. The discipling and baptizing of adults should never be an extraordinary thing in the church. It is part of its ordinary function and ministry.

On the negative side again, the proper discipling and baptizing of adults does not in itself exclude the baptism of infants who belong to the covenant setting of faith, proclamation, and prayer. The distinction which arises here must not be erased. The children of confessing Christians, although they share the guilt of the race and need the common reconciliation, are not in the same position as pagan children. To ignore this is to run contrary to biblical fact that is plainly basic to the life of the Christian community. The rule of adult baptism applies in its own sphere but does not eliminate the parallel rule of infant baptism.

As a final point on the negative side, no support has been found for the idea that baptism is a sign, witness, or expression of what the baptized person does, even though that person be an adult making the required profession of faith. Profession of faith certainly is to be seen as a prerequisite but it is not the thing signified in and by the sign. Nor is there any obvious biblical basis for the notion that baptism is a first, symbolic step of Christian obedience. Indisputably, following an ordinance is obedience, but that is not to say that expressing obedience is the point of the ordinance. Not committing murder is obedience, but the commandment has its own content and significance apart from the obedience expressed. To link the meaning of baptism merely to what the recipient does by way of faith, obedience, or discipleship hardly seems to be in line with the profound theological presentation of it in Holy Scripture.

When we consider the positive aspects we find first that the baptism of infants in a covenant setting is consonant with God's dealings with his people in both the Old Testament and the New. This does not prove, of course, that infants have to be baptized. Parents are not disobeying any clearcut command if they withhold baptism from their children. On the other hand they are assuming that the extension of the covenant promise to the nations has brought a discontinuity with God's mode of covenant dealing with families and peoples. No evident support can be found for this in the New Testament. Indeed, all the evidence that we have points the other way. Christians still live within a family structure and a church structure. The one covenant of grace still obtains. The covenant signs have been changed, but they still are signs. The types of baptism continue to bear witness to God's work in family and people. The church is the Israel of God but not to the exclusion of God's Old Testament people and not as its spiritualization.

We also find positively that baptism, like the word itself, bears first and final testimony to the work of God on which any response of our own must be grounded. If baptism tells us what we ourselves are to do, it bases this imperative on the indicative of what God has done, does, and will do for us. Hence baptism does not arise *out of* any work of ours. It is baptism *into* the work of God on our behalf. Naturally, if no knowledge of this work is available, baptism can have no meaning. For this reason its administration is dependent on the presence of the word which tells us of the divine work. Adult converts from unbelief are baptized when the word has come to them and they have heard and received it. Their children are baptized because they are already in the sphere of the word and are to hear it as soon as possible. They belong to the people of the word. The electing, reconciling, and regenerating work of God forms the basis of their life and the primary theme of their upbringing. Since the word which tells of this work is with them from the very first, they may properly receive the sign, seal, and testimony of God's sovereign activity before them, for them, and in them.

Also positively, we find that even our own response is the work of God. In this area two points can easily be overlooked. The first is that regeneration is not a human possibility, and the second that it does not stand alone but is part of that total renewing in Christ's image which embraces sanctification and glorification as well. When these truths are appreciated, the difference between adult and infant baptism is set in its proper perspective. It is relativized both by the distinction between divine and human possibility and also by the discrepancy between human achievement and divine purpose and perfecting. Even the adult has neither reached that which baptism signifies nor begun to grasp what its consummation will be. By coming to personal repentance and faith he may be a little further on the road of entry into the divine work. But the Spirit who has brought him thus far is the Spirit who works in infants too—and both he and they have a long way to go before they are brought by the Spirit into the fullness of the baptismal work.

On the positive side we see finally that children cannot

be denied a part in the divine work of salvation. The witness of scripture is surely conclusive enough here. If, then, baptism signifies what God does in election, reconciliation, and renewal, infants who enjoy the thing signified cannot properly be denied the sign so long as they are brought up within the covenant and with an assurance that they will hear the gospel promises. This does not mean automatic salvation for the baptized any more than it means automatic perdition for the non-baptized. What it does mean is that salvation extends to infants too and that where the means are present by which the Spirit does his gracious work of calling the sign of salvation may also be extended.

Like every practice of the church, infant baptism can be poorly administered, and when it is, grave abuses ineluctably follow. Since a proper use will naturally conform to a proper theological understanding, it might be helpful to close with some simple practical guidelines which are implied in the present exposition.

1. Since no direct mandate of infant baptism exists, no absolute rule of infant baptism should be imposed on a congregation. This has often been done, causing unnecessary dissension in the church. When parents have conscientious scruples about baptizing their children these scruples must be respected, although a place should be found for quiet discussion to see if the scruples are as well founded as perhaps at first sight they appear. Is it too much to hope that all churches, Baptist included, might provide freedom of this kind with the opportunity, not for contention and propaganda, but for calm scriptural and theological deliberation?

2. In view of the biblical significance of baptism, churches should not give, and their members should not expect or request, a repetition of baptism when some first

or new experience of the work or gifts of the Holy Spirit is enjoyed. Instead, they should be taught more effectively the meaning of the baptism they have as the sign and seal of the saving work of God and thereby be led to see in any new experience the fulfillment of this work and of baptism as its sign. God is one, the covenant is one, the people of God are one, and the work of God is one. So, too, baptism is one. There may be many experiences as we enter into God and his work, but there cannot be many baptisms, only a richer identification with that which baptism signifies.

3. Christian parents should be ready for a more serious commitment to the spiritual upbringing of the children they bring to baptism. More is demanded than simply sending them off somewhere for a little instruction. Authentic commitment will involve prayer, concern, teaching at home by word and work, and an environment of worship and hearing God's word. Through these means of grace the Spirit does his regenerative work. It is farcical, then, if the Spirit is invoked in baptism but the means of grace are neglected.

4. Church and minister have a responsibility as well as parents. They have this first at the disciplinary level. While no purpose is served by setting up an inquisitorial and self-righteous system, effective pastoral ministry should be available to promote genuineness of commitment in members. This will mean the elimination of those who patently have only a peripheral connection except where there is hope of giving it a deeper reality. It will certainly mean a clear understanding that infant baptism should not be sought except where the prerequisites are met and the obligations are seriously undertaken.

5. The responsibility of church and ministry also arises at the level of Christian nurture. Parents should not be

expected to act alone here. Nor should the church leave a gap of time before measures are taken to bring baptized children under its ministry. Baptism needs to be followed up at once by congregational action. Child care should be available so that continuity may be maintained in worship and witness. Ongoing prayer for the baptized ought to have a place on the prayer agenda of the congregation. The greatest possible effort is demanded in the bringing of children to the knowledge of God and his saving work. With the children all members need to learn the meaning of their baptism. Since its covenant setting embraces the community as well as the family, neither must be left to work in isolation from the other.

6. Finally infant baptism, as we have seen, ought never to be viewed as the ordinary pastoral situation in distinction from the extraordinary missionary situation of adult baptism. The mission of outreach constitutes an "ordinary" part of the ongoing work of the church, and as new people are brought in from the outside the baptism of converts ought regularly to accompany the infant baptism which comes from within the congregation. Only weak theology and poor administration can produce the unhealthy situation in which a vast majority in loosely christianized areas will be baptized in infancy. When the church clarifies the issues of faith and discipleship, and apostasy helps to bring them into sharper focus, a constant need for adult baptism will arise. Far from being a threat to infant baptism, this will serve the better to bring out its meaning. Similarly infant baptism, when properly given, can prevent a subjective misunderstanding of adult baptism, not invalidating it, but referring it to its true and only basis in the electing, reconciling, and regenerating work of the Triune God of which it has its primary significance as the sign and seal.

Indexes

I. SCRIPTURE REFERENCES

OLD TESTAMENT

SCRIPTURE REFERENCES

II. SUBJECTS